A Bite-Sized Public Affairs Book

The BBC – At 100
Will It Survive?

Edited by

John Mair

Cover by

Dean Stockton

Published by Bite-Sized Books Ltd 2021

Bite-Sized Books Ltd Cleeve Road, Goring RG8 9BJ UK information@bite-sizedbooks.com

Registered in the UK. Company Registration No: 9395379

ISBN: 9798533769174

Contents

Section Two:
A 360 degree panorama on the Diana Panorama.

Section Three:
Current and future affairs

Acknowledgements

This is the fourth in my Bite-Sized 'BBC In Peril' series. My sixth hackademics collection on the subject in the last decade. Each time the storm clouds gathering over new Broadcasting House have got darker. The attacks on the Corporation grow from all sides day by day. One of our great British cultural inventions maybe in existential danger. It needs an 'NHS moment; the Johnson government bears it ill.

I hope I am wrong and that their 'whack' goes elsewhere.

These books – this is my forty first hackademic tome – are collective efforts. They are turned round in record time-this one in eight weeks – and that can only be achieved through the enthusiasm, dedication and talent of the authors. Twenty in this volume. None are paid. Nor am I. I thank them profusely.

Others too. Bite Sized Books new and old. My old friends Julian Costley and Paul Davies and their new efficient editorial manager Steven Polywka made it happen. Phil Barnes made the online launch sing. Neil Fowler stopped calumnies of grammar and style with some super subbing. My wife Susan allowed me use of the family dining table and fed me physically and emotionally!

I thank them all. Enjoy the book. Let it be food for thought and action by all sides.

John Mair Oxford England July 2021

Foreword/Prologue

Tim Davie; The History Boy

An unusual perspective on the 17th Director General of the BBC. Sir Anthony Seldon the very distinguished contemporary historian , the former Vice Chancellor of the University of Buckingham and Brighton and Wellington Colleges recalls one of his charges in his very first teaching job.

I'm looking at a black-and-white photograph from May 1984 of a row of lower sixth formers looking as if they're straight out of Alan Bennett's play, set in Thatcher's decade, *The History Boys.*

Courtesy of Sir Anthony Seldon

The photo was taken at Beaumont Hamel memorial park to the north end of the Somme battlefield, preserved in memory of the Newfoundland soldiers slaughtered on the first day of fighting.

I had taken the boys, from South Croydon's Whitgift School, to France for the weekend with my wife Joanna. The aim was to deepen their understanding of the war for a production of *Journey's End* I was directing at the end of term.

School teachers can be dewy-eyed about the first cohort of students they encounter. I had joined the school, my first teaching job, the previous September, and maybe I am a bit biased. But to me they were, and still are, a very special group of young men, and I enjoyed their company.

As a thank you for the trip, they gave me a cassette of Dire Straits' *Making Movies* and a rapidly framed photo taken from the street in the early hours of Sunday morning of them waving and doing non Ofsted-approved things out of the Arras Hotel windows. They'd remembered I'd liked *Tunnel of Love* which they played in the back of the minibus on the journey, and I think the picture was an apology to Joanna and me for waking us up in the middle of the night when the double bed on which they had all been sitting broke in two in the room above us at 3am.

Didn't they do well?

I have never worked out why some of those I taught went on to do exceptional things while others faded into the suburbs, leading good lives bringing up families away from the limelight. Those I most expected to go on to take commanding positions, the heads of school and the big characters, often did not. Indeed, it's not uncommon for former head boys and head girls to experience emotional and mental difficulties after they leave school.

Tim Davie was a nice lad, but not a stand-out. Born in April 1967 into a relatively modest home in Purley, his father was a wine and spirit salesman and his mother a psychiatric nurse and teacher. His parents divorced when he was eleven, BBC historian Jean Seaton reminding us that he was not the only BBC Director General to grow up without a father figure at home. Quite possibly, it held him back at first, but built his resilience and made him more determined when he began to find his feet.

The young Tim was bright, and won a half scholarship to enter Whitgift School aged 13 in September 1980. His first three years saw him work diligently for his 11 O-levels: his reports show that he was conscientious and likeable if un exceptional. One of his teachers records him working hard, but reluctant to show how conscientious he was. But then most hard-working teenage boys are like that.

9

Sabre rattling.

Fencing was the activity that saw him first blossom. Whitgift was a strong fencing school, second only in the country to Brentwood. Tim became secretary of the fencing club in his lower sixth year, and captain in the upper sixth, performing as First Sabre and First Foil in the school team, and coming fifth in the national school championships at Crystal Palace in 1984-85.

Fencing master, and later headmaster, David Vanstone, recalls Tim started fencing later than many, his determination and commitment ensuring he made up ground on those who had started fencing two years earlier. Vanstone recalls him as unusually focussed, absorbing quickly the technical guidance in lessons and never forgetting what worked. Sabre, he says, was Tim's weapon of choice, and though slight in physical terms he fenced so fluidly and with such technical accuracy that he became the obvious choice for Captain. He remembers him being very popular, taking other boys with him and leading by example and encouragement - the others in the team thought he was 'a great lad who gave his all'.

Teenage journalist and Thespian

Tim was already making a name for himself when I joined the school. My first encounter with him was on the school magazine, which I edited, and I made him 'deputy general editor'. With a team of budding journalists, our modest aim was to redesign it from ground up, and make it more striking and stimulating than any similar product in the country. The editorial team had long, mad, weekends staying up till late moving round bits of text and images stuck on with 'cow gum' (a wonderful device which disappeared in the 1990s with the advent of computers).

Drama was his other big interest. Apart from *Journey's End,* he acted in *Oliver* and *Peer Gynt,* directed by legendary headmaster David Raeburn, whose final report had this to say:

'A lively actor who has regularly appeared in School productions and an active contributor to our cultural life in other ways, especially as a member of the editorial team which has totally revitalised our school magazine...'

Tim threw himself into *Journey's End*, acting with volume and some style But what I remember most was something else. He believed his brother, two years younger and struggling with aspects of the school, might benefit from being in the play company. An artist, he asked if he might design our set (which he did with flair), and come with us on that anarchic trip to the

Somme and Ypres. Throughout. Tim watched over him with brotherly love and insight. I was struck by it at the time, and I am struck by it as I recollect it nearly 40 years on.

Making it to Cambridge-by the skin of his teeth?

I lost sight of him in the last few months of the upper sixth when his head was firmly on his A-levels (History, English and Business Studies) and I wasn't teaching him. He steadily strengthened academically, and set his heart on reading English at Cambridge, so was devastated that August to learn on holiday in Cornwall he had achieved only three Bs (and a top grade in English S Level). In despair, he phoned his English teacher (another future head, Andrew Grant) and said 'that's it: I'm off to Nottingham'. But Grant told him: 'prove you want Cambridge by reading some plays and delivering me an essay on Shakespeare by the time you get back home. If you do I that I will back you'.

A life-changing conversation. Essay delivered, Grant indeed backed him, and four months later, Selwyn College Cambridge offered him a place to read English. Grant recalls him as: 'very capable without being flashy; courteous, quite earnest and modest, so when I heard about his appointment as DG, I dared to think they might actually have got it right'.

Cambridge scholar…and DJ

So, like his fellow history boys Mal and Alan, he made it into Oxbridge. Once there, he came into his own academically and personally, developing his confidence and entrepreneurial interests, not least as a DJ. The clues to his future ambition can be found far more in his post-18 life than before. Some who scaled the heights, Richard Branson or Boris Johnson, revealed their precocious talent and ambition when still at school. Davie did not.

But those early formative years reveal him to have been a conscientious, creative and compassionate young man, traits which, I believe, he has never abandoned. They are exactly what the BBC will need in the Davie decade if it is to survive and reimagine itself beyond its centenary.

About the contributor

Anthony Seldon's book *Impossible Office: the History of the British PM* was published in April 2021.

Section one.
Timewatch: BBC History lesson

Introduction

John Mair

As the centenary of the BBC approaches in October 2022, there will be much *sturm und drang* not least from the BBC itself. Like measles it will be all over the radio and television schedules. We have asked three of Britain's more distinguished media academics to celebrate and cogitate.

Brian Winston, the Lincoln professor at the University of Lincoln is a former programme maker-*'World in Action'* amongst his credits-before entering the portals of the academe. He deserves a medal for this contribution. It was partly written in an intensive care unit to which he had been admitted. Great journalists never miss deadlines even with surgical gowns on.

His piece- *It is to make no picayune point to ask exactly what 1922 broadcasting centenary is being celebrated in 2022* is perceptive. Professor Winston has delved into the archives and thinks any celebrations are premature. They should happen in 2027 one hundred years after the British Broadcasting *Company* became a *Corporation.* His genesis of the birth of radio through war and of the BBC through commercial interest makes for fascinating reading.

Professor Paddy Barwise is an acknowledged academic authority on modern public service television. He and Peter York have setup a BBC Defence Army though their book *The War Against the BBC: How an Unprecedented Combination of Hostile Forces Is Destroying Britain's Greatest Cultural Institution… And Why You Should Care.*

Paddy looks to the bible for inspiration for his piece -*Auntiegeddon: Will the Philistines Finally Destroy the Temple Built by John?* on BBC early history

All have a role in this fable. John Reith is John the Baptist from Stonehaven.

'And there came unto them a mighty man named John, five cubits of stature, an engineer from North Britain and a son of the manse and servant of God. And John said unto them, I will lead the company, and I will hire the best engineers in the land to build the transmitters and studio, even as you ask. But God hath not sent us these wonders just to play cheap dance music records'.

Yet the brilliant temple he and others built has philistines at the gate today. They are numerous.

'Many, although not all, of the BBC's enemies are, indeed, 'philistines' – at least in their attacks on it – ignoring its central role in our national culture and creative industries. They include politicians, think tanks and newspapers, some individual authors, endless websites with names like *Ban the BBC* and *TV Licence Resistance*, and the 'astroturf' (artificial grassroots) #DefundTheBBC campaign' History repeats itself with the BBC. Often.

Finally, Professor Sylvia Harvey of the University of Leeds. In '*Uncharted Seas': the BBC's Passage to the Twenty First Century she* considers the relationship between the government and the BBC in the 1920s and during the Suez crisis and hopes for a more mature relationship in the twenty-first century.

The BBC failed the first BIG test-the 1926 General Strike. Tens of thousands of workers out in support of the coal miners. Which side should the BBC take? Reith's view was that whilst the Company should remain as independent as possible in order to maintain a level of trust from all sides in the conflict, nonetheless the BBC should be 'for the Government in the crisis'. In simple language support the status quo. That position did not go down well with the Labour movement who lost that strike.

Once again in 1956 the nation was divided. This time over the invasion of Suez. This time the BBC position was more nuanced. The Labour Opposition leader Hugh Gaitskell was offered airtime

Moving on to the contemporary scene, the waves are still choppy. Bashir is the latest storm over the BBC following on from Jimmy Savile, Lord McAlpine and Sir Cliff Richard. They blew over eventually. It was Reith himself who used the metaphor of 'uncharted seas' in his 1924 book *Broadcast Over Britain.* In the new millennium the BBC has encountered both icebergs and opportunities and has to some extent 'made its own weather'. Forecast at present variable!

Chapter 1

What 1922 broadcasting centenary is being celebrated in 2022?

Professor Brian Winston, a former broadcasting hack turned distinguished academic, delves into the archives and discovers that the BBC may be premature in celebrating its centenary in 2022

1922. Certainly, in that year, on 18 October, a commercial British Broadcasting Company, was formed and then registered at Somerset House (15 December). It was dissolved three years later (31 December, 1926) and liquidated three years after that (12 December, 1929). It was, legally and constitutionally, a quite distinct sort of entity from the British Broadcasting Corporation, established by the medieval governance device of a Royal Charter of incorporation. which came into existence on 1 January, 1927:

'George the Fifth, by the grace of God, of the United Kingdom of Great Britain and Ireland and of the British dominions beyond the Seas King, Defender of the Faith, Emperor of India. All to whom these presence shall come Greeting!

......whereas it has been made to appear to us that more than two million persons in our Kingdom of Great Britain and Northern Ireland have applied for and taken out licenced to install and work apparatus for wireless telegraphy for the purpose of receiving broadcast programmes ......'Anon (Royal Charter) 1927.

In consequence: 'a decision has been made after due deliberation to recommend that the broadcasting service hitherto carried on by the British broadcasting company limited... be conducted by a public corporation acting as trustees for the national interest':

The British Broadcasting Corporation – The BBC.

So, just when was the BBC born?

In our received history and the BBC's official archive, these two events have been elided:

'The company was formed.... by a group of leading wireless manufacturers (a.k.a. 'the radio trade') in discussion with 'politicians, and the press; negotiations with the Post Office; attempts to deal with programming policy through public representation (Broadcasting Board); views on programmes and opinions expressed by shareholders '(Anon.BBC Archive Hub),

Buried in this list of players being consulted, however, lies an obfuscating distortion, viz: that it involved '*negotiations* with the Post Office'.

The fact was that, without the GPO (aka 'the Government'), 'the radio trade' would simply not have existed. They operated transmitters, catering for a growing market of 'receive-only' listeners (also holders of GPO licences but with no voice). The listed parties were called together at the behest of the Post Office. The commercial company concept reflected the state's need to deal with an elephant in the corner room.

The genesis of steam radio

For several centuries, the concept of representative democracy had been emerging and central to it was the exercise of the right of free expression (under the law). Here, though, for the first time, with radio, was an expressive communication medium which utilised a limited natural resource – the electro-magnetic spectrum. The investigation of electronic phenomena – a common-place activity in the world's advanced physics laboratories throughout the 19th century – had already yielded an instantaneous wired communication system: telegraphy.

The possibility of a Speaking Telegraph was understood and subsequently, by the 1870s, emerged as telephony, a second instantaneous and quickly pervasive system. By then, it was also well understood that radiation could allow for these two possibilities to operate without wires.

Wireless telegraphy was first demonstrated as a viable communication system in 1895 during the summer manoeuvres of the British and Imperial Tsarist fleets. By then warships – 'dreadnoughts' – had become so large that fleet deployments put rear flotillas below the horizon scannable by the vanguard. The flags would no longer serve. The signal – 'CDQ' ('Come Damn Quick') soon internationally shortened in morse to 'Save Our Souls' – quickly became a given of life at sea.

In 1905, ships' wireless operators in the North Atlantic were startled to hear, coming from their morse telegraphic loudspeakers, music. Radio had arrived; but for what supervening social necessity remained an open question. It presented one gaping deficiency: as compared with the privacy of telegraphy and telephony, anybody in earshot could listen to the wireless.

Commercial exploitation faltered but the land armies during the World War I utilised wireless as the basis of mobile battlefield communications. By the War's end, enough ex-army wireless operators, all more than capable of using transmitter/receivers (transceivers), existed to constitute a primary market.

The US Federal Government – like all states, its natural proclivity to monopolise military technology – began licencing these transceivers.

Finally, the penny (or, perhaps better, the cent dropped). The point of the radio was, exactly that anybody could listen. The manufacturers continued to produce transceivers and sell them to hobbyists to play with them; but others too, more professional – the press, educational institutions – were also interested in the new medium's possibilities and receive-only – 'cat's whiskers' – devices were being generally marketed as the latest 20th century wonder consumer durable. Programming, such as it was, was, as it were, given away with the purchase of a set.

Not all clear signals

The result, though, was cacophony. Because the physics of radiation worked to produce the strongest signals around the centre of the spectrum at 100 metres wavelength, all transceiver licensees wanted to use it. So, there was a further need for state intervention to allocate specific positions on the spectrum. The potential conflicts around perceived restrictions on free expression, exacerbated in America because of the First Amendment to the Constitution, was dealt with the brilliant ploy of laying off responsibility for content onto the licensees. Censorship became a matter of self-regulation and the elephant was placated. Moreover, with a matching brilliant brainwave, mercantile non-hobbyist broadcasters realised they had a saleable commodity: airtime.

In Britain, the same plot produced a very different story. The GPO had successfully insisted that both telegraphy and telephony were extensions of its centuries' old monopoly over the infrastructure distributing the mails. Furthermore, apart from the military mindset, it also now had the added argument of avoiding the cacophony. (Indeed, the American experience figured large in the British discussions which led from Company to Charter.) Moreover, in the UK, the receive-only sets also required a licence, such additional tax revenue being, of course, irresistible.

Company or Corporation?

To all intents and purposes, then, the potential difficulties with the principle of free expression were simply side-stepped, buried in the obscurantism caused by ignoring the profound legal, and indeed constitutional, differences between the British Broadcasting *Company* and the British Broadcasting *Corporation*. After all, the manufacturers were scarce apostles of Miltonian or Lockean notions of freedom. Other potential programme providers – the press most obviously but also, for example, the theatre etc – were equally happy to have what was a widely believed to be a serious competitor in the offing curbed.

2LO calling

The Company's first station – in London, call-sign 2LO – came on air in November, 1922. Deaf to the right of free speech and blind to the distinction between allocative and regulatory functions, the British Postmaster General (PMG) of the day was quick to take upon himself an unprecedented degree of state-prior constraint. He announced in the House of Commons early in 1923 that in his view: 'it was undesirable that the [radio] service should be used for the dissemination of speeches on controversial matters' – by which, his actions were to demonstrate, he meant, e.g., mentioning the Treaty of Versailles without prior Foreign Office clearance. He did not even allow his Cabinet colleague, the Chancellor of the Exchequer air-time to outline details of the budget (Briggs, 1995: 54-55;243-245).

The mealy-mouthed justification for such action was that it was not de facto censorship but merely exerting a 'positive influence'.

Not because of free expression issues, but rather because the sales of sets were not producing sufficient anticipated revenue, this arrangement could not be final. So, still ignoring the fundamental constitutional problem, the immediate uncertainties which were emerging were resolved by a Committee of Inquiry which guaranteed the monopoly until 1926. Sales picked up ('two millions of persons in my kingdom' and financial stability was achieved. Nevertheless, out of the PMG's hands, a fuller scale Committee (Crawford) was appointed by government with a remit to re-examine the whole issue.

The tax on listening confirmed

Crawford produced the arguments leading to the determination that radio's technological exceptionalism required an exceptional response, viz: the creation by Royal fiat of a publicly funded (via the hypothecated tax that was already in place as the receive-only licence fee) of a non-commercial monopoly to provide programming to the British people. It came on air on 1 January, 1927 and, listening to radio, no-one much noticed that the 'C' in BBC now stood for a *corporation* and not a *company*. Crawford left the company's operational organisational arrangements pretty much in place.

The times in general must be remembered. This was the Roaring Twenties and post-WW1 social unrest and dislocations were everywhere. It was an era of polarised politics, of revolution even. Beglamouring technicism, reinforced by radio's emergence as a platform for propaganda, was, without much real evidence, assumed to exert unprecedented mass media influence over its listeners. In Britain, even as Crawford was reaching his conclusion in the summer of 1926, a General Strike – mild by comparison with events elsewhere – was seen by the authorities and the middle class as a pre-revolutionary crisis. This was not a moment for a consideration of arcane constitutional issues.

And, post-1927, whatever else can be said, the BBC's record of public service to the preservation and enrichment of the country's cultural life (albeit perhaps at a cost of super-serving middle-class expectations) has been extraordinary. Its performance during World War II remains an unmatched model for mass media conduct in times of extreme social crisis and conflict. But there has been a cost and the institution that they, and we, continue to pay for it.

Supporting government

During the days of the 1926 General Strike, as Crawford was winding up, senior members of the British Broadcasting Company news operation betook themselves to the offices of the government's main PR department, setting Milton, Locke and all their legatees spinning in their graves.

So, perhaps the best use we can make of the 1922 centenary is to remember why today's institution-in-being is actually only 95 years old and how the confusion masks an essential problem which has yet to be addressed. Could be, we have five years in which to properly seek a resolution to the conflict between allocation and the regulation of expression which has been festering since the off.

Otherwise, by 1927 we could well be remembering that our failure so to do was the BBC's hamartia.

About the contributor

Brian Winston, the Lincoln Professor at the University of Lincoln, began his career on Granada TV's *World In Action*. As an academic, he was the founding director of the Glasgow University Media Group (*Bad News; More Bad News*) and is the author of *A Right to Offend, The Rushdie Fatwa and After,* etc. Winston's latest book (Matthew Winston, co-author) is *The Roots of Fake News: Objecting to Objective Journalism* (2020).

References:

Anon (BBC Archive Hub): 'History of the BBC' (citing doc: GB 898 BBC/CO1).

https://www.bbc.com/historyofthebbc/timelines/1920s [accessed 28 June 2021].

Anon (National Archive) 1927: 'Royal Charter for the BBC'
https://www.nationalarchives.gov.uk/education/resources/twenties-britain-part-two/royal-charter-for-bbc/ [accessed 28 June 2021]

Briggs, Asa (1995). *The History of Broadcasting in the United Kingdom: The War of Words*. Oxford. Oxford University Press,

Chapter 2

Auntiegeddon: Will the Philistines finally destroy the temple built by John?

The Gospel according to Paddy Barwise. The guru of academic writing on the BBC delves into biblical history to find a frame for the current attacks on it

Queen Vic had reigned for three score years, when there came into the land a wizard, Mar-Koni. And the wizard sent signals through the air, even over great oceans. And all were amazed.

And the years passed, and the wizard showed that one signal could be received by great multitudes, if they had the equipment.

And in the twelfth year of the reign of George, the son of Edward, the son of Vic, there came companies that made reception equipment for the wizard's signals. And their leaders said, 'Great is the wizard, for now we can flog equipment to everyone so that, wherever they dwell, from the End of the Land even unto John O'Groats, they can receive the signals.'

And then they said, 'What signals? We must hire a servant to build a company with great transmitters and a studio and someone to play dance music records or something, that the people will purchase our equipment.'

And the company's signals shall be scattered across Britain, even as the sower broadcasts seed over the ploughed field. And therefore shall it be called the British Broadcasting Company.

And they did advertise for a servant to lead the company, and to build the transmitters and studio and hire people to play the dance music records.

And there came unto them a mighty man named John, five cubits of stature, an engineer from North Britain and a son of the manse and servant of God. And John said unto them, I will lead the company, and I will hire the best engineers in the land to build the transmitters and studio, even as you ask. But God hath not sent us these wonders just to play cheap dance music records.

And John had been wounded in the Great War against the Huns, and he was strong of spirit, voice and body, fierce of countenance and quite scary. So, although they felt in their hearts, 'What's the problem with cheap dance music records if the people like them?' (a question many still ask), they hearkened unto his words.

And he said, I will build a great temple to broadcast the signals. And it shall inform and educate the people, not just sell them your equipment, and play just a few dance music records if they be not blasphemous and delight not in fornication. And its message shall be one of peace. And above its great portal shall be written, 'Nation shall speak peace unto nation'.

And mayhap God caused the leaders of the companies to be befuddled but, as in a miracle, they hired John and let him build the temple even as he said, and it still stands after nearly a hundred years.

Enough. Reith is such an Old Testament figure that the King James Bible[1] language seemed irresistible. And there really is something miraculous about his appointment.

His 'temple' is our greatest cultural institution and source of global 'soft power'. And, despite huge consumption and technology changes, ever-growing competition and cuts of over 30 per cent in its real funding since 2010 in a market with rising real costs, we Brits, on average, still use it for over two hours a day – and, globally, it reaches over half a billion people a week. So, who are the 'philistines' trying to destroy this temple, what arguments do they use, and will they finally succeed?

Who are these Philistines?

The biblical Philistines who fought Benjamin Netanyahu's ancestors probably came from the Aegean to the southern coast of Palestine, which is named after them, around 1200 BCE. But 'philistine' in the modern sense (materialistic and lacking intellectual and artistic understanding) was first used by seventeenth century German students to describe 'townies'.[2]

Many, although not all, of the BBC's enemies are, indeed, 'philistines' – at least in their attacks on it – ignoring its central role in our national culture and creative industries. They include politicians, think tanks and

---

[1] Another of the glories of Britain, commissioned by another Scot and the only great book ever written by a committee – and a committee of academics too.
[2] 'Philistine', *https://merriam-webster.com/dictionary/Philistine*. The first use of 'culture war' ('kulturkampf') was also in Germany, referring to Bismarck's clashes with the Catholic Church.

newspapers[3], some individual authors, endless websites with names like *Ban the BBC* and *TV Licence Resistance*, and the 'astroturf' (artificial grassroots) #DefundTheBBC campaign.[4]

Some, like Rupert Murdoch, have a clear vested interest in diminishing the BBC: 'Ye shall know them by their fruits'.[5] Others, like the Institute for Economic Affairs, are driven more by ideology: 'Father, forgive them, for they know not what they do'.[6]

Although the BBC has critics on the left (especially for its reporting on the prophet Jezza) and the centre (mainly for its Brexit coverage), large-scale, non-stop Beeb-bashing comes overwhelmingly from the right. There are several possible reasons for this imbalance: commercial vested interests are mostly on the right; right-leaning organisations tend to be well (and opaquely) funded; and most British newspapers – who also largely set the broadcast news agenda – lean right. Finally, the BBC's right-wing critics often mistakenly think almost everyone else agrees with them – the 'silent majority' illusion.

What arguments do they use?

The BBC's enemies have long claimed that it is untrustworthy, left-wing and, now, anti-Brexit and 'woke'. Many people agree, especially if they themselves are right-leaning, socially conservative, older and pro-Brexit. But almost as many (typically younger and left-leaning) people think the opposite, while a large minority in-between see it as broadly impartial. And asked which *one* source they turn to for news they trust, 51 per cent of Britons say the BBC – far more than for the second-ranked source, ITV (9 per cent). Fewer than 4 per cent choose *any* of the anti-BBC papers.[7]

---

[3] Not great fans of Matthew 7 (motes, beams and all that). There's a vast gulf between their constant Beeb-bashing and their recommendations of what to watch and listen to, and their celebrity coverage, much of which features BBC programmes and personalities. Their hypocrisy comes into sharper relief when there's a scandal like the 1995 *Panorama* interview fiasco: their coverage suggests that Diana's death had nothing to do with paparazzi.

[4] See Barwise and York, *The War Against the BBC*, pages 272-5, for the evidence on #DefundTheBBC's charming claim to be 'just a kid with a laptop frustrated at the way the BBC conducts themselves'.

[5] Matthew 7: 16.

[6] Luke 23: 24. Whatever the question, the IEA's answer is *always* the same: leave it to the market. However, despite being primarily ideological, it also has a financial vested interest in spreading free-market propaganda, since at least some of those providing its funding, such as the tobacco giants and US farming interests, have a clear commercial interest in deregulation, lower corporate taxes, and all that.

[7] The *Sun*, *Mail*, *Express* and *Telegraph* ('Smet' for short). Source: Ipsos MORI for the

Other claims are about money: the BBC's alleged inefficiency, wastefulness, excessive size, scope and market impact ('crowding out' commercial media) and the idea that many people don't use its services but are forced to pay the licence fee or go to prison. These are all pretty much complete nonsense. Similarly, Lord (Ian)Botham's recent claim that "In 2015, Tony Hall announced that, in return for a big increase in the licence fee, the BBC would pay for all pensioners aged over 75. Tony Hall then broke that promise"[8] packs *three* factual errors into 32 words.[9]

Will the Philistines finally succeed?

The BBC is far too popular for its enemies to destroy it overnight. But by relentlessly cutting its funding, they'll gradually turn it into an irrelevant sideshow like PBS in America – unless and until the public realises what's happening and stops them. So, not the end of days yet – there's still time to avoid Auntiegeddon.

About the contributor

Patrick Barwise (https://www.patrickbarwise.com) is emeritus professor of management and marketing at London Business School and former chairman of the consumer organisation Which?. He joined LBS in 1976 after an early career at IBM and has published widely on marketing and media. His latest book, co-authored with Peter York, is:

The War Against the BBC: How an Unprecedented Combination of Hostile Forces Is Destroying Britain's Greatest Cultural Institution… And Why You Should Care (Penguin, November 2020).

BBC, April-May 2019. See Barwise and York, page 241.
[8] Patrick Sawer, 'Lord Botham: Over-75s "incandescent" with BBC in wake of Martin Bashir scandal', *Daily Telegraph*, 1 June 2021.
[9] The 2015 licence fee settlement cannot by any stretch be called a 'big increase' in the licence fee. It was agreed that, 'subject to charter renewal', the licence fee would merely increase in line with general (CPI) inflation – not in line with the rising real cost of content and distribution – and with deep top-slicing. Second, the BBC did not agree to 'pay for all pensioners aged over 75'. It agreed to *take responsibility for* the free TV licence scheme. So Tony Hall and the BBC Board did not break any promise. Forced to choose between (A) deep service cuts, while limiting the free TV licence concession to poorer households with one or more members aged 75+ (using the Government's means-tested Pension Credit as the criterion of need) and (B) even deeper service cuts while maintaining the concession for all households with over-75s, regardless of household size or income, the BBC Board chose A. This decision was entirely within the terms of what was agreed in 2015.

Chapter 3

Uncharted seas: The BBC's passage to the 21st century

Professor Sylvia Harvey considers the relationship between the government and the BBC in the 1920s and during the Suez crisis and hopes for a more mature relationship as this new century develops

In 1921 a group of radio manufacturers in Britain banded together to create a new kind of service, one that might encourage purchase of their still unfamiliar devices (Briggs, 1961: 125). The first General Manager of the British Broadcasting Company, an engineer and former soldier, John Reith, was appointed in December 1922; though the first broadcasts of the company had commenced a few weeks earlier.

During its early years the output of this novel business succeeded in its intended purpose – the selling of more and more radio devices. A more substantial future was envisaged as the government devised a scheme for selling obligatory licences for the use of the device and, more importantly, passed on part of the income thus generated to the company to meet the costs of increasingly ambitious programme-making (Briggs,1961:106).

The battle over news

Broadcast output was closely supervised, nowhere more so that in the arena of news where the company was advised or even required to avoid reporting on major controversies. On this issue there was ongoing tension and argument between Reith and the Postmaster General; the Post Office at that time being the government department charged with supervising this experiment in public communication.

If the government was often anxious, the press were hostile, fearing an existential threat to their business. In 1923, in an effort to extend the remit of the Company Reith attempted persuasion thus: 'Great discretion has to be exercised... but if on any controversial matter the opposing views were stated with equal emphasis and lucidity, then at least there can be no charge of bias.' (Scannell and Cardiff, 1991:27).

The company becomes a corporation

Following much debate and evidence gathering by various Parliamentary Committees it was finally decided in 1926 that the privately-owned *Company* should become a public *Corporation*. Reith was a persuasive figure, eventually counting among his friends both the then-Prime Minister Stanley Baldwin and the Archbishop of Canterbury, Randall Williams (the latter baptised Reith's son in 1928) (BBC, 2021: John Reith).

In December 1926 Reith was granted a knighthood and from the 1 January 1927 he became the first Director General of a new organisation, the British Broadcasting Corporation, operating under the rules outlined in the BBC's first Royal Charter. This 'new' BBC now operates under its ninth Charter, valid until December 2027.

The General Strike and the BBC

Subsequent critics and supporters of Reith have seen the nine day-long General Strike of May 1926 as providing the key testing ground for the already quite tightly constrained British Broadcasting Company. The Postmaster General had been the most senior politician overseeing and arguably controlling the output of the fledgling company; though Reith had argued consistently for the right to maintain a meaningful level of independence.

The strike was caused by the imposition upon the mineworkers of a longer working day, along with a reduction in wages (National Archive, Cabinet Papers, 1926). As the unionised printers, along with railway and other transport workers, had been called out on strike by the Trades Union Congress the British Broadcasting Company became suddenly and unexpectedly an important source of news and information.

While other newspapers appeared intermittently if at all, the government published its daily *British Gazette*, edited by Winston Churchill then Chancellor of the Exchequer and using his role to take a very strong line against the strikers.

It is important to note that the strike itself was a big national event and that the events of the Soviet revolution of 1917 and the subsequent civil war and execution of Czar Nicholas II (cousin to Britain's King George V) remained relatively recent memories. How would the Broadcasting Company respond?

Reith's view was that whilst the Company should remain as independent as possible in order to maintain a level of trust from all sides in the conflict, nonetheless the BBC should be 'for the Government in the crisis' (Briggs, 1961: 332). Nearly 100 years after these events, assessment is perhaps coloured as much by a sense of cultural norms as by political preferences. It might be astonishing, therefore, to 21st century sensibilities to learn that the relatively less hawkish Prime Minister, Stanley Baldwin (compared with his Chancellor of the Exchequer), not only broadcast a message to the nation from Reith's own house but included in it some wording supplied by Reith himself: 'I am a man of peace. I am longing and working and praying for peace, but I will not surrender the safety and security of the British Constitution' (Briggs, 1961: 331).

Such views expressed from the comfortable homes of upper-middle class London cut little ice with those desperate for change and for a better standard of living. In a letter to the *Radio Times*, published after the strike had ended, the Member of Parliament for Middlesbrough, Ellen Wilkinson, expressed her anger:

'The attitude of the BBC during the strike caused pain and indignation to many subscribers. I travelled by car over two thousand miles during the strike and addressed very many meetings. Everywhere the complaints were bitter that a national service subscribed to by every class should have given only one side of the dispute. Personally, I feel like asking the Postmaster General for my licence fee back'. (Cited in Scannell and Cardiff, 1991:33)

Permission to speak?

Members of the Opposition Labour Party had asked to speak about the Strike and Reith, as Managing Director of the Company, had passed on this request to government 'strongly recommending that they should allow it'. However, as he records in his then private Diary, the request was turned down (probably in part because of a tension at Cabinet level between the Prime Minister and his Chancellor of the Exchequer):

'I do not think that they treat me altogether fairly. They will not say we are to a certain extent controlled and they make me take the onus of turning people down'. (Briggs, 1961: 344)

Reith was clearly not willing to jeopardise his own position or what he saw as the future prospects for the Company and, specifically, the opportunity to become a public Corporation supported by a Royal Charter (to operate from January 1927).

It seems therefore fair to conclude that during the events of May 1926 the power of government, combined with the compliance of the BBC's leadership, contributed to a negative outcome for Labour and trade union interests. The views of the workers on strike were not permitted direct expression on the airwaves. Messages from the TUC's General Council 'continued to be broadcast throughout the strike' though the BBC's historian Asa Briggs also notes that one internal message sent to Station Directors outside London recognised that there would be '…a certain natural bias towards the Government side'.

To this Reithian observation Briggs adds his own comment regarding the class experience of those then working for the BBC – there was 'no doubt that the straight facts of working-class life were not well known to most members of the early BBC' (Briggs, 1961: 340; 342).

Conflict over Suez

Thirty years later, at the time of the 1956 Suez Crisis – when the BBC was already safely into its fourth Charter – the Corporation provided an opportunity for the Leader of the Labour Opposition in Parliament (Hugh Gaitskell) to speak on equal terms with the Conservative Prime Minister (Anthony Eden). Though this was a very different kind of conflict and there was clearly a deep division both within Britain and in Parliament about the wisdom and even the legality of a British military intervention in Egypt seeking to restore the pre-eminence of British commercial interests in respect of the use and control of the great Canal (Briggs, 1995: 73-157; Mills, 2016: 83-7; Gaitskell, 1956; Eden, 1956).

Navigating the 21st century

Many of the political tensions faced by the BBC in its early years have continued well into the 21st century, despite the general rise in incomes and expectations that followed in the wake of the Second World War.

It was Reith himself who used the metaphor of 'uncharted seas' in his 1924 book *Broadcast Over Britain*. In the new millennium the BBC has encountered both icebergs and opportunities and has to some extent 'made its own weather'. Since 2008 it has encountered the effects of a global financial crisis, and a 30 per cent reduction in the value of its licence fee, followed in 2020 by a global pandemic and an existential threat from a hostile Conservative government (Barwise and York, 2020; VLV 2020).

Delivering a public service

There have been considerable achievements including the invention of *Freeview* (assisting millions of homes to make the transition from analogue to digital broadcasting with an exclusively free-to-air service) and of the *iPlayer* (making broadcasting fit for the online era) and negotiating a ninth Royal Charter to run for eleven years from 1st January 2017 to 31 December 2027.

In 2019 *BBC One* continued to be the most popular TV channel with a share of 22 per cent of total audience, compared with an *ITV* share of 18 per cent (*Broadcast,* 6 March 2020: 26). *Sky Sports Main Event* took a 1 per cent share of total audience (BARB, 2020: 29). Regarding the take-up of *Freeview* this service was present in 4.6 million UK homes in 2004 but this had risen to 17 million by 2020. By contrast in 2020 the *Sky* satellite subscription service had 8.4 million subscribers with Cable attracting 4 million (Harvey, 2021; Ofcom, 2005: 246; BARB 2020).

In conclusion, and as the BBC seeks to position itself as both a broadcaster and an online provider, it is worth querying the 'inevitabilism' of the theory of a necessary transition from broadcast to online delivery. In 1924 Reith wrote of the discovery of broadcasting that it is:

'...a reversal of the natural law, that the more one takes, the less there is left for others... the broadcast is as universal as the air. There is no limit to the amount which may be drawn off. It does not matter how many thousands there may be listening; there is always enough for others when they too wish to join in... Most of the good things of this world are badly distributed and most people have to go without them. Wireless is a good thing, but it may be shared by all alike, for the same outlay and to the same extent... (Reith, 1924: 217-218)

Reith grasps here one of the key and perhaps original features of broadcasting – that it can offer limitless access to shared ideas, surprises, sounds and images. Spectrum must be allocated and resources must be found to build a transmitter network and to invest in good quality content. But free-to-air broadcasting has the advantage of offering (unlike social media) a form of communication that can be simultaneously and widely shared in real time.

It is thus, arguably, a more social form of communication, not limited to the one-to-one, point-to-point structure of the internet. As social media and online subscription video on demand grow rapidly it would be a mistake to think that these forms can replace broadcasting; just as broadcasting cannot replace them. (Sandvig, 2015; Harvey, 2016).

About the contributor

Sylvia Harvey is a Visiting Professor in the School of Media and Communication at the University of Leeds. She studied for her doctorate at the University of California, Los Angeles and has published on film history and policy, the political economy of the media and on broadcasting policy and regulation. She is a founder member of Sheffield Doc/Fest.

References

BARB (2020) 'Tracker Households by TV Platform' at: **https://www.barb.co.uk/trendspotting/tv-landscape-reports/** Accessed on 25 June, 2021.

Barwise, P. and York, P. (2020) *The War Against the BBC. How an Unprecedented Combination of Hostile Forces Is Destroying Britain's Greatest Cultural Institution...and Why You Should Care.* London: Penguin Random House UK.

BBC Trust/Budd Report (2007) *Report of the Independent Panel for the BBC Trust on impartiality of BBC business coverage.* London: BBC. Available at: **https://www.bbc.co.uk/bbctrust/our_work/editorial_standards/impartiality/business_n ews.html** Accessed on 25 June, 2021.

BBC (2021) History of the BBC. 'John Reith: Corporation Man 1927-38' Available at: **https://www.bbc.com/historyofthebbc/research/john-reith/corporation-man/** Accessed on 24 June 2021.

Briggs, A. (1961/ 1995) *The History of Broadcasting in the United Kingdom. Vol. I The Birth of Broadcasting 1896 – 1927.* Oxford: Oxford University Press.

Briggs, A. (1995) *The History of Broadcasting in the United Kingdom. Vol. V Competition. Oxford:* Oxford University Press.

Broadcast (2020) *'Channel Overview', 6 March, p.26.*

Eden, A. (1956) BBC History: 'Anthony Eden, Prime Minister, 3 November 1956' [Televised speech]. Available at: **https://www.bbc.co.uk/programmes/p07t36gr** Accessed 25 June 2021.

Gaitskell, H. (1956) BBC History: 'Hugh Gaitskell, Leader of the Labour Party, 4 November 1956' [Televised speech]. Available at: **https://www.bbc.co.uk/programmes/p07t37px** Accessed 25 June 2021.

Harvey, S. (2016) 'Above Us the Sky. The New Battle for Borders in Spectrum Allocation', pp.63-76, in *Crossing Borders and Boundaries in Public Service Media. RIPE @ 2015*, eds. G. Ferrell Lowe and N. Yamamoto. Goteborg: Nordicom.

Harvey, S. (2021) *Public Service Providers: A New Role for Public Service Broadcasters in the Online Era. A response to Ofcom's Consultation on Small Screen, Big Debate, March 2021. Ofcom's Fourth Review of Public Service Broadcasting (2014-20)* at: **https://www.ofcom.org.uk/__data/assets/pdf_file/0025/218275/harvey-prof-s.pdf** Accessed 25 June 2021.

Mills, T. (2016) *The BBC. Myth of a Public Service.* London and New York: Verso.

National Archive (2021) 'Cabinet Papers. Strike build up' at:
https://www.nationalarchives.gov.uk/cabinetpapers/alevelstudies/strike-buildup.htm
Accessed 24 June, 2021.

Ofcom (2005) *Communications Market Report*. **https://www.ofcom.org.uk/research-and-data/multi-sector-research/cmr** (follow link to National Archives).

Sandvig, C. (2015) 'The Internet as the Anti-Television. Distribution Infrastructure as Culture and Power', pp.225-245, in *Signal Traffic. Critical Studies of Media Infrastructures*, eds. L. Parks and N. Starosielski. Urbana: University of Illinois Press.

Scannell, P. and Cardiff, D. (1991) *A Social History of British Broadcasting. Volume One 1922-1939 Serving the Nation*. Oxford: Basil Blackwell.

Voice of the Listener & Viewer (2020) *VLV research shows a 30 per cent decline in BBC public funding since 2010*. Available at: **https://www.vlv.org.uk/news/vlv-research-shows-a-30-decline-in-bbc-public-funding-since-2010/** Accessed 25 June, 2021.

Section Two
360 degree Panorama on the Diana *Panorama*

Introduction

John Mair

The Bashir crisis in summer 2021 is the biggest and deepest I can remember in my forty plus years of working for and writing about the BBC. It goes to the very heart of its journalism-the 'inform and educate' part of Lord Reith's brilliant mission statement. If the journalism is shoddy and fake, then the trust disappears and with it a big raison d'être for the BBC itself.

In this section we put a 360 degree Panorama on the Bashir Diana *Panorama.*

First up, a true broadcasting intellectual Mark Damazer, the former Controller of Radio 4.A friend of the BBC but still one aware of the imperfections .In *Don't be horrid about the BBC* he fends off the 'woke' left wing charge 'There is a debate to be had about BBC journalism and social liberalism, that most people who work for the BBC would be in favour of gay marriage, a woman's right to choose, against the death penalty, and so on. As would most journalists on the Mail. As would most graduates…'.

David Elstein is no long -term friend of the Corporation. He criticises the BBC about Bashir on many grounds based on his experience as Editor on the ITV *Panorama* me too *This Week*. In *The Bashir Affair: Real and false trails*, he sees slackness and an absence of editorial control, in the discovery of Bashir's deception, modus operandi and cover up

'A series of BBC managers struggled with the prospect of having to tell the Board of Governors that the much-vaunted scoop had been secured by an initial act of deception, committed by a self-confessed liar and fraudster. Comforted by the hand-written note, Tony Hall, the head of news and current affairs, chose to tell the Governors that, despite a 'lapse', Bashir was 'honest and honourable'.

Away from the broadcasting one man think tanks there are those who study the British press week after week. In *'Let he who cast the first stone' The British press, the BBC and Bashir* Liz Gerard, an acerbic commentator, is scathing about Press reaction to Lord Dyson's report but places blame firmly back on the Corporation 'The *Panorama* scandal was, according to the BBC, the work of one "rogue reporter". The subsequent investigation was shoddy; it beggars belief that, confronted with evidence of Bashir's lie after lie, the then head of news Tony Hall should have concluded that he was essentially an 'honourable man'. And heaven knows what the Beeb was thinking of to re-hire (and subsequently promote) Bashir in 2016'

Dorothy Byrne admired the BBC from afar in her role as head of news and current affairs for nigh on two decades at Channel Four-their main competitor in serious broadcasting. In *Bashing the BBC from a liberal perspective.* she pulls few punches in her verdict on some of those who knew the truth and hid it from the Governors and, WORSE, the licence fee payers. 'This scandal has undermined public trust in a great institution. The BBC is supposed to be an upholder of truth whereas it lied and covered up. Bosses may have thought they were protecting the BBC but they were damaging the BBC by going against what it stands for and in fact protecting only themselves, and a dishonest journalist'

Caroline Thomson was firmly in the belly of that BBC beast. Chief Operating officer to DG Mark Thompson and acting DG herself for a while she has scaled the managerial summits of the Corporation. In *Trust post l'affaire Bashir* she centres on trust and loss of it as a result of Bashir's antics and the wider ranging effects on the ecology of British broadcasting and wider.

'This is, as we all know, a critical moment for public service broadcasting as it faces unprecedented competition and unusual political pressure. The BBC, through its governance, has a duty to maintain the trust of the British people. And, whatever our governments might think about the advantages of being able to communicate directly with voters, the existence of a trusted medium connecting mass audiences with their leaders is crucial to the strength of democracy'

Media commentator Paul Connew, a former tabloid editor, in *Centenary celebrations in the shade* says the British national newspapers could not believe their Beeb bashing (their default position) luck with Lord Dyson's coruscating report.

'It took 26 years to finally arrive but when it did it came gift-wrapped and decorated with the bright red ribbon of outrage. Lord Dyson's report into Martin Bashir's legendary *Panorama* interview with Princess Diana was the equivalent of manna from heaven for the BBC's political and media enemies'

From a different perspective Robin Aitken is a former BBC employee now turned severe critic, mainly in the house journal of that tendency *The Daily Telegraph*. In *The BBC at 100: Rightly under threat?* he sees the BBC as making its own misfortune by creating an army of opponents who see 'bias' in all it does especially over Brexit.

'In reaction to this perceived long-term bias, a strong lobby, bitterly opposed to the BBC, has now emerged. This lobby, which comprises Conservative politicians and their supporters, believe that the BBC stands in ideological opposition to them and in recent years they have campaigned against the licence-fee privilege'

Professor Julian Huxley is no Conservative.In *Self-created hostages to fortune* he also says the BBC has made its own bad luck. Not just the Bashir *Panorama* but more recent mis-steps such helicopter door-stepping Sir Cliff Richard during a police raid. Thar proved legally expensive and embarrassing.He blames the Corporations' pursuit of a tabloid press agenda .'One of the paradoxes here, of course, is that press which the BBC sometimes seems so keen to ape is also the Corporation's sworn enemy. But perhaps if the BBC competed less with newspapers on their own terms, they might regard it as less of a rival and moderate their hostility somewhat'

Finally, a BBC Brahmin turned reflective academic .Leighton Andrews was BBC Head of Public Affairs then rose through office in the Welsh cabinet to a berth in Cardiff university. In *The BBC and the end of the 'good chap' culture* he recognises that UK political culture has changed with the populist Boris Johnson and his huge Commons majority. The BBC needs to follow.' What we are left with is the reality of state power in the hands of people whose routine justification is the realpolitik of the people's will. A strong, impartial and independent BBC is sorely needed. At the Commons hearing in June 2021, one MP suggested that the current Prime Minister had been sacked from a newspaper (naming the wrong one, in fact) for doing less than Bashir got away with. That shows how exposed the BBC is on issues of honesty, trust and impartiality. The era of the good chaps is over, and the BBC needs to be better than them and squeaky-clean'.

The storm over The Bashir Affair is no summer squall.

Chapter 4

Don't be horrid about the BBC

The point about the BBC is not that it reaches fewer people today, but that it continues to reach so many, according to former Controller Radio Four Mark Damazer

The power of the BBC has declined, is declining and will decline further. There are obvious reasons for this – and it cannot simply be put down to ideological hostility, poor regulation, weak policy-making, declining resources, or even, heaven forfend, BBC managerial incompetence and journalistic mistakes. There are other large forces that surround the BBC and weaken it.

That was then

In the late Thatcher era, there was a seminar in Downing Street where a young economist observed that the British public was about to discover that it was getting its media on the cheap. A technological revolution was coming, and there was plenty of room for money to pour into British broadcasting, expand choice and return big profits.

At that point there was no satellite TV, pretty well no cable, no internet, no digital anything. It didn't take long for Sky to arrive – and hats off to Rupert Murdoch for the entrepreneurial insight and investment.

This is now

Now we enjoy *Netflix* at £120 a year for a standard subscription, *Amazon Prime* £96 a year, the *Disney channel* £60 a year, *Apple* £180 , a *Sky* package of sport and entertainment – in my case, £600 a year. And so on. By way of comparison, the licence fee has just gone up – to £159 a household. About 44p a day.

And in exchange for your data – at a price you cannot conceivably be expected to work out – you have *Facebook, Twitter, YouTube, Instagram, Google News*, and on and on.

The BBC's total market share has inevitably fallen – particularly among the under-35s. Some individual elements, such as the *iPlayer or BBC News Online*, have grown – the *BBC iPlayer* had 5.8billion requests to stream programmes in 2020 – but the BBC could not have held on to the share of the media market it enjoyed 20 years ago or anything like it.

The BBC's current share of the media market in *broadcasting* comes out at around 30 per cent – far from negligible, but not exactly the behemoth described by its enemies.?

For those who once saw the BBC as a suffocating presence in British life and argued that it should be cut back, there is now the joyful prospect of arguing precisely the reverse case. Why should the BBC get all this money when it is less watched and listened to by the public it purports to serve.

In real terms, the BBC licence fee is at least 30 per cent smaller than it was in 2010. The last two George Osborne-designed licence fee settlements have taken a toll on the BBC's commissioning power. There have been cuts everywhere, including BBC News.

100 not out

And yet. The BBC, coming on for 100, is nowhere near out for the count. The public is obliged to pay but not to watch, listen or log in. But they do. It's a decline, but a decline from what now seems an unimaginable height .

The adult reach of the BBC – the number that use the BBC with some regularity during any given week – is in the region of 90 per cent. About 45 million people a day consume it.

People don't have to do this. The BBC continues to try to please them – as Lord Reith would have it, to inform, educate, entertain – and they continue to come. (The Reithian triad is one of the best mission statements in history. I once sat on a group charged with trying to improve it. Think of *W1A*. Thankfully, after a single meeting, we gave up).

If you were to indulge in an act of vandalism and destroy the rest of the BBC, the last bit left standing would be BBC News. It is the core of the enterprise.

TV in general remains the most-used way UK adults get their news (75 per cent), more than the internet (65 per cent), more than the radio (42 per cent), more than print newspapers (35 per cent). The BBC is the most-used news source: ITV is second, *Facebook* third. The BBC has seven of the top 20 most-used news sources, the highest audience reach (77 per cent), and is the most commonly followed news organisation across social media sites.

The story for news in the nations and local news is the same. The BBC stands at the top, with astonishing figures for audience satisfaction.

More than just facts

All these numbers matter, but it's not only about numbers. The key words for anyone who works at any level for BBC News are independence, impartiality, trust. These are not always straightforward to define – nor are they easy to achieve if you add another desirable ingredient to the mix: quality.

When I was on the BBC Trust, we fretted over the survey results on impartiality. They are weaker than they were. Yet if you look at where the public goes in big moments – elections, Covid, royal set pieces – the BBC tends to romp away. The BBC's coverage of the Duke of Edinburgh's funeral was watched by more than 13million people – and that's a conservative figure – five times as many as opted for ITV.

One way of explaining the BBC's weakening impartiality scores is to consider that they are not a reflection of the performance of BBC journalists, but rather that the BBC, the national broadcaster, suffers the most on this score when the nation is particularly divided and fractious.

Brexit politics was unusually bitter and long-lasting. Doubtless, there were tens of millions who took moderate positions, or for whom the whole thing was a Westminster and media circus, but for tens of millions it was an emotional question of great significance.

Brexit's ability to mobilise passions carries across to views of the BBC's coverage, If you felt strongly about the issues, you reacted strongly to seeing and hearing so many people on the other side. And that applies to Remainers and Brexiteers alike. The UK was awash with anger,

A 'woke fiefdom'

There is a debate to be had about BBC journalism and social liberalism, that most people who work for the BBC would be in favour of gay marriage, a woman's right to choose, against the death penalty, and so on. As would most journalists on the *Mail*. As would most graduates.

But it's a jump to go from there to say that the BBC on air is a woke fiefdom incapable of demonstrating fairness to those who worried, for instance, about immigration, and that the BBC must be "out of touch".

"Specimen A" wheeled out by those who make this case is, of course, Brexit.

The polls had suggested a not very big win for Remain. The BBC reported that, along with everybody else. The polls were wrong – but not crazily wrong. Brexit won by just under 4 per cent. But some Brexiteers seem to think that by *reporting* the imperfect polling, the BBC was *endorsing* Remain. Had the polls been more accurate and if Remain had won, would that have meant the BBC's journalism was by definition good and impartial? Of course not.

The "out of touch" charge risks banality. The apparently "woke" BBC that worries aloud about diversity (not such a bad thing to fret about) and the singing of *Rule Britannia* at last year's Proms is the same organisation that gave you endless hours about the Duke of Edinburgh in the days after his death – abolishing the planned schedule for 24 hours and even forbidding Radio 3's audience its Saturday night date with Stravinsky. Or the organisation that broadcasts *The Antiques Road Show, the Annual Festival of Remembrance* and much else that does not strike a modish note.

The UK is a rumbustious, pluralist democracy where people disagree about many things. There are some moments where there is an overwhelming tide of opinion in one direction – think wartime – but it's not the norm. It would be wrong for the BBC editorial panjandrums to sit around, define a national mood and organise its journalism around it. Rather, the aim is for the BBC to reflect the pluralist mess and use journalistic resources to describe, analyse and test policies or actions that have importance.

Social media is not an echo chamber?

And so, what of *Twitter and* Facebook et al? Outrage is a currency. It drives up usage and it sells advertising. Finally there is a common understanding that *Facebook* and *Twitter* cannot be treated as mere platforms. Those algorithms have massive editorial meaning.

The conventional analysis of the relationship between political polarisation and social media is that social media sites are bubbles where you can luxuriate in your own world view, without being exposed to people who have a contrary world view.

I think the opposite may apply. That you post a view and are confronted by people disagreeing with you in ways that are crude, polemical, often abusive, or worse. It's being exposed to *that* which makes you angrier.

The BBC's interactions with *Twitter* have caused it trouble. Several BBC journalists have been too enthusiastic to write pithy comments that they would not broadcast in the same form, or to endorse other people's tweets in a way that left them open to an attack on their impartiality.

The BBC has been rooted for decades by the importance of fairness, being open to multiple viewpoints, and not having prescriptive opinions about policies. It is not rooted in how many people are following a BBC journalist on *Twitter*.

A lie is a lie?

Once you start using the word "lie", you have to aim for some consistency. Keir Starmer was unlikely to have been telling much of the truth two years ago when asked what he thought of Jeremy Corbyn as leader of the Labour Party. Did he lie?

The New York Times and *The Washington Post* felt that Trump was so egregious a liar that he had to be called out in terms. But the BBC is not a great liberal newspaper. The fact that it shows some linguistic restraint irritates many, but a quick burst of popularity in some quarters is no recipe for reputation in the long run.

None of this is about stopping *contributors* coming on air and accusing people of lying or cheating or swindling, allowing for libel laws. The BBC is not censoring strong expressions of opposition, but it's not for the BBC itself to adopt this tone.

The BBC's audiences include tens of millions of people for some of whom it is the only source of news. They pay the licence fee. Broadcast news and current affairs has its own grammar and has to be judged accordingly. But, within its limits, there *are BBC* quality issues.

The BBC is not all perfect

Here's a sample. I would like to see better use of evidence, a wider range of sources and greater sophistication with numbers. *More Or Less* on Radio 4 is an exceptional programme in which Tim Harford's team picks apart nonsense about PPE or test and trace or so-called medical breakthroughs. Although venerated within Radio 4, its techniques are not transferred to other programmes.

The BBC Trust commissioned a report about the BBC News' use of statistics five years ago. There has been some progress but it's still nowhere near good enough. And there is only occasional experimentation with form.

The BBC has done poorly over decades in using its foreign correspondents to provide an angle of vision on what goes on in the UK. What do we get on Germany or France?

41

Were the Covid stories about understandably grief-stricken families a little too repetitive? And potentially anaesthetising?

The BBC is under incessant scrutiny and is properly accountable in a way that *Facebook, Twitter* and *Google* are not. Even its defenders accompany their views with a desire for reform, though there is not much agreement about the shape it should take.

But the old verities are the right ones. There's no definition of impartiality that is any improvement on the BBC's historic understanding of it. It is better to risk being seen to be unfashionable than to compete with the Piers Morgans and Foxes of this world. One of the sad effects of Fox's rise in the US was its impact on CNN. CNN became a vehicle for angry Democrats. News anchors editorialised at will, fuming about Trump at every turn.

Could BBC News programmes be more fun? More mischievous? More dynamic? I dare say. They are not the central verities. News is a serious matter. That much the BBC understands.

A version of this piece appeared in the June 2021 issue of the British Journalism Review.

About the contributor

Mark Damazer is a former controller of BBC Radio 4 and a former BBC Trust member . He was previously deputy director of the BBC's news division. He was master of St Peter's College, Oxford and a visiting fellow at the Reuters Institute for the study of journalism.

Chapter 5

The Bashir Affair: Real and false trails

Was the farrago twenty-five years later over the 1985 Diana *Panorama* interview avoidable? David Elstein, the former editor of ITV's *'This Week'*, their *Panorama* me-too, thinks the BBC's checks and balances failed

The headlines are all too familiar. The BBC has been exposed as having deeply unsatisfactory internal processes for investigating problems. Rival media organisations gloat over the inadequacies. Loyal BBC employees squirm with embarrassment. We have seen it all before.

The issue this time is the notorious interview with Princess Diana 25 years ago, conducted by Martin Bashir, a junior reporter on the BBC's illustrious weekly current affairs flagship *Panorama*. The programme attracted 23 million viewers, but a retired Supreme Court judge, Lord Dyson, has issued a devastating verdict on how the interview was secured – indirectly, by deceit and trickery – and on how the internal inquiry into that deceit, once it was exposed, was handled: in a 'woefully ineffective' fashion

Lord Dyson's remit did not include two other relevant issues: first, why BBC managers chose to ignore their settled protocol on how to seek royal interviews, and secondly, why Bashir was rehired by the BBC as a religious affairs correspondent long after the facts of his deception in obtaining the Diana interview had become known, not least to the man who had investigated his behaviour in 1995 and had become Director-General by the time Bashir returned to the BBC.

Why ignored the rules?

The first of these issues – by-passing established rules – was at the time treated as something of a triumph of enterprise over convention. For reasons never explained (and his death leaves the questions unanswered), Steve Hewlett, the much-respected editor of *Panorama* in 1995, made two controversial decisions.

He agreed to let Bashir hi-jack a running discussion between the BBC and Buckingham Palace as to when and by whom Princess Diana might agree to be interviewed (she was known to be keen to have her say, after her husband had confessed to his adultery in an *ITV* programme two years earlier). And when Bashir managed to secure a meeting (on his own and with no producer present) with Diana's brother, Earl Spencer, where he presented him with faked bank statements suggesting his former head of security was being secretly paid by a newspaper and the secret services, Hewlett strongly vouched for Bashir to Spencer, who had phoned to check his credentials.

The faked documents, and the promise of more revelations, were enough for Spencer to arrange a meeting with Bashir and his sister. There he regaled them with dozens of bizarre (and mostly invented) stories of betrayal and espionage that persuaded Spencer to regard Bashir as a fantasist (he immediately cut off dealings with him) but persuaded his sister that Bashir was a true friend. To maintain the sense of "us against the world", Bashir arranged with Diana to film the interview in extreme secrecy: it proved to be an explosive encounter.

I cannot think of any instance in which a reporter on a major current affairs series would be authorised to commission graphics from a freelance designer. That is invariably the job of the producer. As soon as Matthias Wiessler submitted his invoice for the fake bank statements, someone should have smelled a rat. What was the project number on the invoice? To whom should the production manager and accountant look to authorise payment? If there was no project number, how could the designer receive payment?

Normal service on a current affairs flagship

I was the editor of ITV's equivalent of *Panorama, This Week*, for four years, and had previously worked on *Panorama* as a director. The structure of both programme teams is very similar. The editor assigns a team of researcher, reporter and producer to each story that is being seriously pursued.

The most senior of the three is always the producer, usually a member of staff, who acts as management's representative throughout. Reporters are usually freelances. That any reporter would be allowed to hold a meeting with Princess Diana and her brother, unsupervised by a producer, should have been unthinkable. After all, what conditions might they seek for granting an interview? What understandings might be reached in the absence of a BBC management representative?

Eventually, a producer was assigned for the recording of the interview itself, but the arrangements for the recording were seemingly controlled by Bashir, and wrapped in extreme secrecy.

With his scoop in his bag, Bashir presented the BBC hierarchy with a dilemma: how much to say before transmission, and to whom. Rather than inform the Board of Governors of the interview (its chairman, Marmaduke Hussey was married to one of the Queen's ladies-in-waiting), Director-General John Birt kept them – and the Palace – in ignorance until just before transmission.

Whether or not disclosure might have risked losing the scoop, for whatever reason, became a moot point. But because of all the subterfuge involved, BBC management became all the more vulnerable when the graphics artist who had been persuaded by Bashir to concoct the fake documents took his concern about whether he had been tricked into a deception to various senior people at *Panorama*. Editor Steve Hewlett's aggressive reaction was to tell all those who raised the issue with him to mind their own business.

The truth comes out. Slowly

When, months later, multiple newspaper stories about the documents forced an internal inquiry, Bashir repeatedly lied about showing the fakes to Spencer, and when he finally admitted having done so, came up with the preposterous story that Diana herself had provided him with the details.

Nor could Bashir come up with any credible excuse for having created the documents in the first place (though he did persuade Diana to send the BBC a hand-written note saying she had no regrets about doing the interview, and had not been shown anything by Bashir that might have misled her).

A series of BBC managers struggled with the prospect of having to tell the Board of Governors that the much-vaunted scoop had been secured by an initial act of deception, committed by a self-confessed liar and fraudster. Comforted by the hand-written note, Tony Hall, the head of news and current affairs, chose to tell the Governors that, despite a 'lapse', Bashir was honest and honourable. Instead, the graphics designer who had blown the whistle would never be employed by the BBC again, and the *Panorama* team members who had raised the matter of the fake documents would be weeded out, labelled as leakers of information to a hostile press.

Then DG John Birt tried to justify to Dyson Hall's extraordinary willingness to take Bashir on trust, on the grounds of the absence of a 'counter-factual': an excuse acerbically dismissed by the judge, who pointed to Earl Spencer as an obvious source of a 'counter-factual, yet who was never approached by any BBC manager for his version of events.

John Ware, a veteran *Panorama* reporter who presented a corrective episode of the show on the day of Dyson's publication identified 'incuriosity' as the fatal flaw in the BBC's management method.

Echoes from BBC history – Savile and David Kelly

In doing so, he echoed precisely the Pollard report on the *Newsnight*/Jimmy Savile failure seven years before. The editor of *Newsnight* had inexplicably blocked coverage of the Jimmy Savile scandal, yet mounting concern about this had seemingly failed to reach the top levels of the BBC, despite widespread newspaper coverage of that concern. For Pollard, the lack of interest by the Director-General (at that time, Mark Thompson) had been matched only by the efforts of those below him to shield him from unwelcome knowledge.

The *Newsnight* Jimmy Savile fiasco was compounded by the programme's attempt to recover lost ground by exposing another paedophile scandal: only for that report mistakenly to identify a Tory peer as a perpetrator, resulting in hefty libel damages, the departure of another Director-General, barely two months into his incumbency, followed not long after by his chairman and the whole Trust structure.

There is a regular element of 'circling the wagons' whenever the BBC finds itself under attack. Acknowledging fault almost never happens, except where an outside agency – with no institutional interests to protect – investigates.

An official inquiry was set up after a government scientist, David Kelly, committed suicide in 2003. He had been identified as the source for a hotly-contested item on the Radio 4 *Today* programme, relating to alleged duplicity in the Blair administration's account of Saddam Hussein's weapons of mass destruction. Lord Hutton's report was scathing about the BBC's editorial processes as well as its seeming inability to admit error.

That episode led to the ousting of the BBC's Chairman and Director-General (Gavyn Davies and Greg Dyke), as well as to the replacement of the Board of Governors by a more distant oversight body, the BBC Trust. Yet the change of governance did little to improve BBC accountability.

Falling over a Cliff (Richard)

The 2015 BBC Charter review saw a combined board of executives and non-executives placed at the top of the BBC: but this proved no more successful than its predecessors when a glaring breach of privacy was committed by *BBC TV News*. Acting on a tip-off to a junior journalist, who used it to pressure South Yorkshire police into reluctant co-operation, the BBC believed it had a scoop when it learned that a flat belonging to Sir Cliff Richard (but in which he had not lived for some time) was about to be raided by police, following up an anonymous complaint of sexual abuse. The BBC deployed a helicopter above the flat, named Sir Cliff as its owner, and ran extensive live footage at the top of a lunchtime bulletin.

No arrests or charges were ever made, and it later transpired that the top BBC managers who took the decision to use the pictures should have known they were unlikely to take place. When Sir Cliff failed to secure a public apology, he sued the BBC, and won overwhelmingly, with the trial judge so dismayed by the BBC's behaviour that he awarded hefty damages: combined with the payment of costs on both sides, the BBC paid out over £2 million when a simple apology would have cost nothing. It was Tony Hall, now Lord Hall of Birkenhead and the BBC's Director-General, who took the decision not to apologise.

Bashir comes home to the BBC

By then, Hall had also nodded through the re-hiring of the proven liar, Martin Bashir, and his subsequent promotion to BBC religion editor. But the growing pressure in 2010 from various newspapers, now briefed by Earl Spencer as to the skulduggery in 1995, was putting mounting pressure on the BBC to hold some sort of inquiry. Hall sensibly relinquished his post in August, and his successor, Tim Davie, asked Lord Dyson to report on what had happened in 1995/6 (though not on later events). If Hall had still been in place, his resignation would have been automatic.

How to avoid disaster

Various ideas are being floated as to how to avoid further such disasters, including a separate BBC subsidiary board, made up primarily of independent editorial experts, to supervise BBC editorial output: the model cited is the main *Ofcom* board and its subsidiary Content Board, chaired by one of its main board members.

There is a much simpler answer: treat the BBC just like any other broadcaster, and make it accountable directly to *Ofcom*. Whatever its other failings (notably, in its oversight of public service broadcasting), *Ofcom* is widely respected for the objectivity and scope of its complaints procedures. It also has powers to order inquiries into broadcaster behaviour connected to the making of programmes. *Ofcom*'s predecessors in the commercial sector – the *ITC* and the *IBA* – had similar powers: the Windlesham/Rampton inquiry into *Death On The Rock* was undertaken at the behest of the IBA (I was the Thames TV Director of Programmes who authorised transmission of that programme).

Broadcasting governance in the commercial sector is both vastly superior to the BBC model, and completely non-contentious as an issue. Why the BBC clings to its long-outdated internal structure is hard to understand: given that *Ofcom* is there as an appeal court anyway, the best the BBC can hope for if a complainant invokes *Ofcom* is that the regulator's response is no different to its own.

The Dyson report is the ideal opportunity for the BBC to embrace the transparency that being accountable to *Ofcom* affords. Next year's mid-term review of the BBC Charter is the ideal moment to grasp that option.

About the contributor

David Elstein is the former Editor of This week and Director of programmes at Thames Television. He was head of programming at Sky Television and the founding CEO of Channel Five,

Chapter 6

'Let he who cast the first stone' The British press, the BBC and Bashir

The Bashir affair may be a nadir for BBC journalism, but is the British press being hypocritical about their own past misdeeds? Liz Gerard casts her forensic eye

When she was in the depths of despair, the tide of publicity turned against her. She was no longer the fairy tale princess, but the royal shopaholic who had lavished a fortune on an endless array of new outfits.

It was she who was held responsible for the steady stream of royal staff who had left their service and it was she who was accused of forcing **her husband** to abandon his friends, change his eating habits and his wardrobe...

At a time when dark thoughts of suicide continually crossed her mind, a *Daily Mail* columnist described her as a "fiend and a monster".'

This passage (with slightly doctored words in **bold**) was written 30 years ago. It refers to Diana, Princess of Wales. But the accusations are remarkably similar to those levelled against Meghan. Duchess of Sussex: selfishness, profligacy, bullying, even the reorganisation of her husband's clothes and diet. In those days it was Nigel Dempster, rather than Sarah Vine or Jan Moir, putting the boot in while a beleaguered woman in a gilded cage considered taking her own life.

Diana spills the beans: 1992

The words are taken from Andrew Morton's book *"Diana: Her True Story",* published in 1992 and updated first to take account of her separation from Prince Charles and then, after her death, to confirm what everyone already knew: this was Diana herself, rather than 'insiders and 'friends' and 'sources' speaking.

I had another read of it when the sky fell in on the BBC over Martin Bashir's *Panorama* interview, bringing everyone – from the second in line to the Throne to the lowest-rent tabloid columnist – out with their bucket of scorn.

The deceit used to secure that interview was reprehensible and the cover-up of the wrongdoing – most especially the destruction of an innocent graphic designer's career – disgraceful. But that doesn't negate the content of the conversation. As she had demonstrated with the stream-of-consciousness tapes she sent to Morton three years earlier, this was a woman desperate for her voice to be heard. She was right that there were 'three people in the marriage'; she was right that, even without that fatal car crash, she was destined never to be Queen. So was she wrong to say she felt isolated in the Palace, that she didn't know how to deal with Press attention, to speak out about her bulimia and self-harming?

'One rogue reporter'?

There is so much in the interview that echoes down the years and is still relevant today – as demonstrated by the whole Harry and Meghan mess – that it should be defended as an important piece of modern history from which lessons can and should be learnt. But instead, the BBC dons a hair shirt and its Press detractors leap on Prince William's demand that it never be shown again. Meanwhile politicians who already have an agenda that includes reining in the Corporation seize the opportunity to kick it while it's down.

The *Panorama* scandal was, according to the BBC, the work of one "rogue reporter". The subsequent investigation was shoddy; it beggars belief that, confronted with evidence of Bashir's lie after lie, the then head of news Tony Hall should have concluded that he was essentially an 'honourable man'. And heaven knows what the Beeb was thinking of to re-hire (and subsequently promote) Bashir in 2016. To judge from the BBC's internal investigation, even the Corporation is baffled.

Press H for hypocrisy

Nevertheless, the sanctimoniousness of the Press has been quite something to behold. In a top leader, headlined "Shocking failure", *The Times* complained that for all their "pious statements of regret" there was no sign that those responsible for "25 years of anguish" showed an understanding of the magnitude of their failures.

Lord Birt, who was BBC Director-General at the time, tried to blame the whole scandal on a "rogue reporter" who "we now know ... fabricated an elaborate, detailed but wholly false account of his dealings with Earl Spencer and Princess Diana". There is no question that Bashir was a rogue reporter. But as Lord Dyson reveals, the BBC was well aware when it conducted its own investigation in 1996 that Mr Bashir had lied to them on three occasions…

Indeed, the BBC's subsequent efforts to cover up for their 'rogue reporter' are as serious a breach of journalistic standards as Mr Bashir's deceptions.

Another 'rogue reporter'

Have we stepped through the looking glass? Wasn't another "rogue reporter" guilty of some dastardly deed related to the royals? Indeed, didn't he go to jail for his actions? Ah yes, Clive Goodman, the *News of the World* royal editor who was convicted in 2007 for hacking the phones of advisers to Princes William and Harry.

News International (now News UK), of which *The Times* was and is a subsidiary, didn't try to cover up for Goodman, but it did "co-operate" with a wholly inadequate investigation that similarly concluded there was no further problem. And where it took 25 years to determine that Bashir did appear genuinely to have been a single 'rogue reporter', it took only four to blow open the News International fiction and reveal that dozens of journalists were complicit in wholesale criminality that disrupted the lives of thousands of innocent people.

Back to that *Times* leader:

'What is particularly galling is that those most culpable have gone on to enjoy successful careers.'

Careers built on?

That would be Tony Hall, who rose to become BBC director-general, a member of the House of Lords and chairman of the National Gallery's board of trustees. He left the BBC last year, but that wasn't enough for *The Times*. 'It goes without saying he ought now to resign,' it thundered of his role with the National Gallery. He duly did.

The editor of the *News of the World* when Milly Dowler's phone was hacked in 2002 was Rebekah Brooks. She was still in that chair when one of her news editors was suspected of plotting with private detectives to discredit an officer investigating a failed murder investigation. She went on to edit *The Sun*, which has just had to pay a reported £500,000 to former MP Simon Hughes for illegal information gathering on her watch.

By the time the hacking scandal broke, she had become chief executive of News International. Her old paper was closed down, but she remained in

51

post for nearly two weeks before resigning with a reported £11m payoff. Two days later she was arrested. She claimed not to have known about the hacking and was cleared of all charges at an Old Bailey trial.

As editor of two national newspapers, Brooks was not sufficiently in control of her staff to know that they were engaging in industrial-scale criminality and almost certainly trying to sabotage a police investigation. She was also apparently unaware that it is illegal to pay police officers for information. Some phone hacking victims might find it "particularly galling" that she is now back in her old job as chief executive of News UK.

Then there was the *Daily Mail,* which had led the charge against Martin Bashir – twenty pages of it on the day Lord Dyson's report was published, including a spread on its own part in the investigation that brought about Bashir's downfall and the BBC's shame. Good stuff. But what about the journalist, the *Guardian's* Nick Davies, who exposed the criminality at the *News of the World*? Surely that was good too? Up to a point, Lord Copper.

In 2011, the *Mail* ran leaders decrying the disgraceful practice of phone hacking, but – to paraphrase – these were the misdeeds of one rogue title; the rest of Fleet Street should not be tarnished by that. Within three years, the *Guardian's* Nick Davies was being denounced in a 3,000-word essay as "the man who did for the British Press".

The *Mail* has always vehemently denied phone-hacking, but the practice was certainly not confined to the *News of the World.* And there are other dark arts that were used widely across Fleet Street – the employment of private detectives (which the *Mail* did extensively), blagging, "blackmail" exclusives where celebrities are cornered into making deeply personal announcements to ward off more damaging "shock exclusives". Ask Kellie Maloney, Phillip Schofield and Gareth Thomas about that.

Diana: The media manipulator? Charles too?

Viewed through the rear-view mirror, Diana was certainly a victim. Newspapers leapt on the assertions by her sons and brother that there was a direct line from the *Panorama* interview to her death. But that's a real stretch, as is the suggestion that the deception that secured the interview influenced what she said once it took place. Earl Spencer described his sister as "a young girl, in her mid -30s" – a couple of years younger than Prince Harry is now. No one seems to be putting what he's been saying of late down to youth or naivete.

Diana knew how to manipulate the media. If she had wanted to stick to talking about land mines and Aids, she could have done so. She knew the message she wanted to get across – and even the Dyson inquiry accepted that she had sent a note to Bashir months later saying that she had no regrets.

And what, exactly, might she not have said? The two quotes everyone remembers are "There were three of us in the marriage" and "I want to be a queen of people's hearts". Her complaints of a cold Palace machine and her description of her feelings of isolation and helplessness had been conveniently forgotten until the whole interview was raked over in the wake of Dyson. Before that, no one thought – or dared – to make the link when Meghan raised the same concerns in her Oprah Winfrey interview and ask: "Is there a problem with the Palace?"

It was the same story when Prince Harry said in a mental health podcast that he had needed to get away to "break the genetic cycle of pain". This was portrayed as a shocking assault on his father and grandmother. But hadn't the Prince of Wales done the same? A year before the Bashir interview with Diana, Prince Charles had a series of broadcast conversations with Jonathan Dimbleby in which he criticised his "harsh" and "hectoring" father and described his mother as distant (and confessed on television to his long-standing affair with Camilla Parker-Bowles).

Both parties had had adulterous affairs; both had had intimate conversations with their lovers tapped. The rancour was there for all to see before the couple separated in 1992 and finally divorced in 1996. To suggest, as Prince William did, that *Panorama* nailed the coffin down on the marriage is absurd. For three bereaved men, the BBC is an easy target for blame that won't bring the tabloid columnists crashing down on them.

As for the Press, what we have here is a shelf full of greasy, fat-encrusted, carbon-blackened pots getting extremely agitated about a bit of ancient limescale on the kettle in the corner.

About the contributor

Liz Gerard spent more than 40 years in newspapers, 30 of them at *The Times,* where she rose from sub-editor to night editor. She started blogging about the Press in 2013 and was a three-times winner at the *Editorial Intelligence* Comment Awards. She now writes and speaks widely about print media and politics.

Chapter 7

Bashing the BBC from a liberal perspective.

Dorothy Byrne is the just demitted doyenne of British television journalism. She headed up Channel Four's news and current affairs for nigh on two decades. She says Martin Bashir was a 'wrong un' but one the BBC knew was in their midst and over-protected.

Nice liberal people are not supposed to criticise the BBC, even when it does something really bad. But it does really bad things sometime and we should say so. If nice liberal supporters of the BBC leave all the criticism to right-wing opponents, we do the organisation no favours. We strengthen the image of the BBC as a smug self-satisfied body whose privileged bosses think they are beyond criticism.

More than a quarter of a century ago, *Panorama* journalist Martin Bashir used fake documents to help win the trust of Princess Diana so she would do an interview with him. That interview was a great success bringing fame, glory and awards to all involved and even some not involved. Then some within the organisation began to ask questions about how the interview was obtained; why had the most famous and glamorous woman in the world given her only television interview to a dull bloke with an obsequious manner whom few had heard of? That's when the creation of the fake documents emerged.

But rather than turn against the faker and hand back all their gongs, BBC bosses told the whistle-blowers to f.. off, condemned the poor graphic artist who had created the documents in all innocence and let Martin Bashir off the hook. Apparently, when Bashir finally admitted he had commissioned the fake documents, he cried. The head of news was moved by those tears and concluded he was an honourable man who deserved a second chance.

Even when the fakery was exposed in the *Mail on Sunday,* the BBC didn't come clean.

From tears to fame and fortune and back again.

That's all bad but now the story gets ridiculous. Bashir went on to fame and fortune, even if some asked questions about how he gained some of his later scoops. He did well at ITV and then hit the big time in the US. There, however, his world came crashing down when he was criticised for making lewd and inappropriate comments about women. But back at home his old employer then helped him pick himself up, very high up. He was appointed religious affairs correspondent of BBC News and then elevated still further to become the Editor of Religion.

When suspicious other journalists asked the BBC, under Freedom of Information law, to reveal any documentation on the original fakery scandal, they were at first told there was none. Well done to dogged journalist Andy Webb who, while making a documentary for *Channel Four*, eventually got the BBC to admit that was untrue and cough up the evidence. Credit where it's due, the BBC then hired a former Master of The Rolls Lord Dyson to carry out an investigation into the sorry affair and published his damning report. They subsequently rather shot themselves in the foot by getting one of their own blokes to carry out a further inquiry into how on earth Bashir got the religion gig. This inquiry found Bashir was appointed because he was the best man for the job at the time. Apparently the internal candidates were not good enough even to reach the final interview stage. They'd be justifying in wondering if maybe the truth was that they were not bad enough.

The BBC way .. and waste.

So, what does all this tell us about the BBC and why does it matter? First off, it's clearly a spectacular example of BBC waste. The report by Lord Dyson cost more than a million pounds. If the BBC had only listened to its own whistle-blowers, that would have been money saved. On *Panorama* at the time, there cannot have been proper editorial oversight and the way in which the whistle-blowers and the graphic artist were treated was not only shameful, it shows how vital it is to have an independent system for dealing with those who blow the whistle.

Those whistle-blowers were perceived to be endangering the reputation of the BBC but in fact they were the defenders of the principles of honest journalism and therefore they were the defenders of the integrity of the organisation. As so often, the cover-up has been even more damaging than the original sin. Let's imagine if the BBC bosses had dealt with the matter differently at the time; sacking Bashir, handing back the awards, and introducing better editorial oversight and an independent hotline for whistle-blowers. It would have been grim but the scandal would have been deep in the past by now and not therefore one to be used against the BBC by those who are calling for the licence fee to be cut or even abolished or for the BBC to be sold off and put behind a paywall. Prince William argues that the lies of Bashir poisoned his mother's mind. Some argue that contributed to events which led to her death in the Paris accident because she had rejected the protection of Buckingham Palace security. That would make the BBC's error a life and death matter. The graphic artist saw his BBC career ruined and the whistle-blowers say their careers were blighted.

'Long Bashir' and too 'posh to wash' journalism.

This scandal has undermined public trust in a great institution. The BBC is supposed to be an upholder of truth whereas it lied and covered up. Bosses may have thought they were protecting the BBC but they were damaging the BBC by going against what it stands for and in fact protecting only themselves, and a dishonest journalist. A number of people have said it's unfair to hold the BBC to much higher standards than are expected of other institutions and indeed pointed out that other organisations have done much worse things. Look at the phone hacking scandal, they say.

But as well as the obvious fact that two wrongs don't make a right, I judge the BBC by higher standards than those by which I judge the *News of the World*. This scandal demonstrates that the instincts of many in any institution are to hide wrongdoing but it's by admitting wrongdoing that an organisation demonstrates its true integrity. The BBC has also shown itself to be an inward-looking organisation. Both the then Director of News James Harding, a former *Times* editor, and Head of Current Affairs Joanna Carr at the time of the 2016 reappointment of Bashir said they hadn't known about the *Mail on Sunday* expose of his methods.

This is the journalistic equivalent of being 'too posh to wash'. No wonder journalists on broadsheets and in the BBC are accused of not understanding the minds of most British people. To understand what is in people's minds, you need to read and watch what they are being filled with, even if you don't like or believe a lot of it.

Ethics and a faker

The BBC decided to give Bashir a 'second chance' but the effect of their naive generosity was to let loose on TV journalism in the UK and the US a man they knew to be a faker. The awards he won for the Diana interview helped him to gain entry into other organisations which must now be wondering what he might have got up to when working for them. The BBC has also failed to investigate properly and transparently a claim by the mother of one of the 'Babes in the Wood' murder victims her claim, backed by a Bashir colleague at the BBC, that he took away her daughter's bloodstained clothing promising to return it after forensic investigation but never did so. Bashir denies taking the clothing but the testimony of the mother and colleague needs to be examined properly.

Tears for souvenirs of the BBC's reputation?

I am struck by the effect of Martin Bashir's tears on his boss. I find people often mistake tears for a sign of remorse. As a former teacher, I am generally suspicious of someone who bursts into tears when confronted with alleged wrongdoing. It is just as often, and indeed more often, a sign of having been caught out. The fact that they fell for his tears is an indication of a naivety. Bashir was undoubtedly a 'bad un' and, in my experience, devious journalists are rare in television. But they exist. In some ways I am shocked by how shocked the BBC have been to have discovered someone bad in their midst. Why should television journalism be the only sphere of life not to attract anyone dodgy? There's a certain ivy towers vanity in their surprise. And their naivety shows they need more street-wise people and fewer posh bods trained in Spinoza and Socrates.

Finally, this scandal shows it's wise never to claim any credit for something in which you have no involvement. We have all been annoyed by people who have claimed a part in one of our hard-won successes. My memory at the time is of a lot of back-slapping among BBC blokes at the time of the interview. Where are they all now?

About the contributor

Dorothy Byrne was Head of News and Current Affairs at Channel Four from 2003-2020.She was responsible for many hours of factual television each and every week. She is now the incoming President of Murray Edwards College Cambridge.

Chapter 8

Trust post l'affaire Bashir

Does the BBC need a new regulatory system following Lord Dyson's report into Martin Bashir's 1995 Diana interview? Former BBC Chief Operating Officer Caroline Thomson considers the arguments

It feels like remote history, but it's true: 27.1 million people watched Boris Johnson announce the first lockdown for the UK on 23 March 2020. The sequel in May, announcing the path out of lockdown, attracted an even larger audience of 27.5 million, while the PM's announcement of a repeat of lockdown in January 2021 drew a slightly smaller audience – as repeats tend to – of "only" 25.2 million.

All three of those programmes represented mass gatherings around our TV sets. Only one event since the advent of multichannel television has surpassed them all: the funeral of Diana, Princess of Wales, in September 1997, was watched by 32.1 million.

It's easy to think that it is only disaster that impels us to huddle around the screen, but the largest TV audience of all time in this country was in fact for a triumph (if you happen to be English). The 1966 World Cup final drew an estimated 32.3 million viewers, according to the somewhat primitive contemporary methods of measurement then used by the BBC and ITV. The opening and closing ceremonies of the London Olympics brought together 24.4 million and 24.6 million people, respectively, in front of their television sets.

Trust, news and power

I dwell on this mass of figures to demonstrate the power of two things: trust and news. There is nothing that drives us to share an instant experience more than the coverage of live events – and nothing that drives our choice of how to watch it more than our trust in public service broadcasters.

That ability to gather people together is an immense power to rest in the hands of corporations and one of the strongest reasons why so many nations choose to have at least one well-funded broadcaster that serves a public purpose. It is also why broadcasting should not be regarded or regulated as an industry like any other, and why it should be – as it is today – given special status for its cultural, social and cohesive value.

In each of these cases I cite, more than half, and up to three-quarters, of those audiences watched on the BBC. The proportion that watched Diana's funeral on the BBC was 60%.

It's hardly surprising that politicians should be suspicious of any organisation that wields that much potential power and influence with the people on whose votes they rely for their own ability to govern.

The BBC under pressure and in crisis – always

The BBC has always had to be aware of that suspicion and the pressure on the corporation's independence that accompanies it.

However, I am not sure the BBC has always responded in the best way, either to allay political suspicion or, by contrast, to resist threats to its special status as an organisation outside the currents of politics.

It is exceptionally good at making television shows, radio programmes, news content; it is a model for other nations around the world in the way that it helps to stimulate the broader cultural health of the UK; it is much less good at being open and accountable about its decision-making and its processes.

The trust bestowed upon the BBC by the British public is hard won and easily lost. It can never be taken for granted. To be relied upon in the future, there has to be greater transparency and accountability. The question is how to achieve this without either exposing the BBC to the perils of political manipulation – something that is happening to an alarming extent in other European countries, from the Netherlands to the Czech Republic – or damaging its ability to compete in a hardening, consolidating market.

To some extent, it is inevitable in an organisation as large and multi-faceted as the BBC that transparency and accountability can suffer when there is a sense of siege outside and uncertainty within. But that is precisely the moment when it is imperative that the processes of openness are working.

For the BBC, crises mean that its critics always reach for the governance button. I am not convinced.

Ways forward? Another committee? No!

There has been a suggestion of appointing an editorial committee to supervise BBC News production. My experience tells me that adding layers of bureaucracy is rarely the way to improve either function or accountability within Broadcasting House. Who would appoint this committee? What would prevent it becoming a tool of politicians and outsiders heavily influenced by the BBC's commercial enemies in the publishing industry?

Or, in the future, by other external forces that we cannot predict today? At its most basic, how do you prevent it becoming yet another tick-box exercise?

An editorial committee with any taint of political appointment, just like a politically-appointed main board, would destroy independence and rot the trust of licence-fee payers.

The BBC's governance and operational problems are, at heart cultural, rather than regulatory. Leadership by example to change that culture for the better and to encourage honest self-reflection and accountability is the key.

In Tim Davie, the BBC has a very strong Director-General more than capable of doing this. I think the process could be helped by the appointment of one – carefully chosen and reliably free-thinking – non-executive director. They would be a guarantor of independence, of editorial standards and of accountability and could have the added advantage of being the designated, obviously independent, recipient of whistleblowers' complaints.

This is, as we all know, a critical moment for public service broadcasting as it faces unprecedented competition and unusual political pressure. The BBC, through its governance, has a duty to maintain the trust of the British people. And, whatever our governments might think about the advantages of being able to communicate directly with voters, the existence of a trusted medium connecting mass audiences with their leaders is crucial to the strength of democracy.

Defence is the BBC default position. Is it right?

It has always suffered from external attacks and thus, I think, adopted a defensive posture more often and more strongly than perhaps it might have done. This in turn promotes secrecy, rather than openness, in any organisation – another reason for putting cultural change ahead of regulation, something that independent broadcasting has had quite enough of already.

Appear on the *Today* programme, answer questions on *Feedback,* use your own airwaves to explain and make your case; but also listen and, yes, when necessary, apologise.

When David Cameron first achieved power by agreeing a coalition with Nick Clegg in 2010, the BBC cut into normal scheduling to show that democratic process in action. The audience – I am back to big numbers again – was 9 million people, 2 million more than would have watched the episode of *EastEnders* that "WestminsterEnders" replaced.

That power inherent in the BBC is the friend of government and people. Responsibly and accountably used, it is a pillar of our communal relationship. But it is a power that belongs to the people, not to parties. It is worth more, and it should be protected more thoughtfully, than the BBC's would-be reformers would have us believe.

This piece first appeared in the June 2021 edition of Television.

About the contributor

Caroline Thomson is the Chair of Digital UK. She was the BBC's Chief Operating Officer from 2006 to 2012.

Chapter 9

Centenary celebrations in the shade

Media commentator Paul Connew analyses how the scandalous tale of one rogue reporter, two humiliated Director-Generals and a sorry trail of cover-ups and incompetence could sabotage the BBC's centenary celebrations. A longstanding defender of the Corporation, he rejected offers to defend the indefensible. A strong believer in public service broadcasting, he found disturbing parallels between the Bashir scandal and another BBC reputational disaster in which he was involved.

It took 26 years to finally arrive but when it did it came gift-wrapped and decorated with the bright red ribbon of outrage. Lord Dyson's report into Martin Bashir's legendary *Panorama* interview with Princess Diana was the equivalent of manna from heaven for the BBC's political and media enemies and the stuff of clickbait orgasm for the 'revoke the woke' tendency, including Andrew Neil's technology-bedevilled curate's egg *GBNews*.

But even for those of us with a history of defending (as well as criticising 'Auntie') it posed the question: How to defend the indefensible?

Yes, it was easy to scent hypocrisy in the reaction of those newspapers still smarting from the BBC's coverage of the phone-hacking scandal and the Leveson inquiry legacy. 'The BBC's greatest day of shame in history' (*Daily Mail*) 'rancid skeleton in their closet-a jaw dropping betrayal of journalist ethics' (*The Sun*), 'the damage to its claim to represent the nation will be hard to repair' (*The Times*) and 'The BBC's continued existence in its current form is bad for the country in a dozen important ways' (*Mail on Sunday*).

Lord Dyson's hand grenade

But who could blame them, given the excoriating and forensic condemnation of Lord Dyson's 127-page report into how senior executives – one of whom became Director-General – 'too readily accepted' Bashir's own version of events to protect an award-garnering global 'scoop' even when they knew fraud, fakery and deception figured in how it had been obtained?

In the case of the *Mail on Sunday,* a fury understandably heightened by the BBC's extraordinary operations to discredit the paper's original stories exposing Bashir's methodology not long after the *Panorama* interview aired. The BBC's tactics back then came in for scathing criticism by Lord Dyson.

'Tabloid revenge' won't wash this time

But attempts to mitigate on the grounds of 'tabloid revenge' don't wash this time. Dyson's most damaging line, arguably, was to convict the BBC of 'falling short of the high standards of integrity and transparency which are its hallmark'.

Journalism professor and *Guardian* columnist Jane Martinson, hardly a member of the BBC bashing print fraternity, was spot on in an article on May 20 headlined *'Trust is key to BBC's survival—so it must learn from Martin Bashir scandal'.*

Wrote Martinson 'In an age of fake or overtly politicised news, the BBC's position at the top of polls for trusted sources of information is its most powerful weapon in the fight for survival against commercial, social and political attack.

'Yet the most dangerous part of Lord Dyson's report is in some ways the section he helpfully called ''Issues that I have not addressed in this report'. Unless the BBC truly addresses them, internally as well as externally, then the allegations that the Bashir scandal was not about a 'rogue reporter' but a cultural indifference will never truly go away. And the BBC is too important for this to happen'.

Siren warnings ignored, just like Savile?

Professor Martinson rightly contended: 'This isn't to say the BBC should not chase ground breaking interviews and exclusive stories—but when its desire to create headlines clashes with siren warnings about methods, things usually go wrong. Different in so many ways, the scandal over Jimmy Savile and the helicopter pursuit of Sir Cliff Richard share an astonishing ability to ignore warning signs'.

Whether the BBC's failures and cover-ups around Bashir are as morally reprehensible as those involving Savile is highly questionable. In timing terms they are certainly more dangerous for its future as 'Auntie' approaches an uncertain 100th birthday 'celebration'.

A declaration of personal interest here. I was the *Sunday Mirror* editor legally thwarted from exposing Savile back in 1994. When details of that became public after his death I featured in a number of BBC programmes, including *Panorama* and *Newsnight,* in which the BBC soul-searched its own failures, and cover-ups. I also testified to Dame Janet Smith's Savile equivalent of the Dyson Bashir inquiry, as well as various police investigations. Several disturbing similarities about the BBC leadership mindset struck me as Bashir unfolded.

The initial refusal of BBC chiefs to face their own cameras, the internal blame-gaming and backstabbing. In my Savile experience, off camera, I was besieged by calls from various senior BBC figures seeking to know who I thought knew what and when about Savile's proclivities within the corporation. In particular there was an obsession over whether my investigations into Savile was the reason his hit show *'Jim'll Fix It'* was mysteriously axed around the same time. To which my answer was, 'No, I haven't a clue but you should!'. Ill treatment and dismissal of whistle-blowers exposed during Savile featured again—shamefully—in the Bashir scandal.

With an increasingly authoritarian, scrutiny-resentful, Johnson government in office the upcoming BBC review and the longer-term charter renewal negotiations to come, the BBC's new Director-General Tim Davie should be bracing himself for the Tory Right seeking to revive de-criminalising licence fee evasion ahead of a concerted campaign to scrap the licence fee altogether after 2027.

Running scared after Bashir

Are there worrying signs of *BBC News* running scared in the wake of Bashir? I was astonished when Commons Speaker Hoyle uncharacteristically and publicly lambasted Boris Johnson for bypassing parliament to announce 'Freedom Day' was being postponed didn't merit a mention on either the BBC's 6 or 10pm flagship TV News Bulletins.(although *Newsnight* later did it justice). I asked a fairly senior executive why and got the private suggestion: 'In the current climate we tend to be careful on negative stories about the PM on news bulletins, call it a kind of rationing if you like'. *Hmmm..*

Is Tim Davie still a Tory?

Davie's own past Conservative party connections won't help much. Boris Johnson, not instinctively anti-BBC personally and hardly a paragon of journalistic virtue, would be likely, if still in office, to sacrifice well-funded BBC independence on the altar of Tory populism.

While Davie deserves credit for the relative speed with which he set up the Dyson inquiry, he deserves less for the subsequent internal one into Martin Bashir's extraordinary re-employment as religion correspondent, and subsequent promotion to religion editor. Suffice to say calling in Ken MacQuarrie, the BBC's long-time internal go-to inquiry man, who cleared all those involved in the original Bashir fiasco of any 'cover-up' while acknowledging bleedingly obvious 'shortcomings' in his re-hiring process has predictably played badly.

If the Dyson report wasn't excoriating enough, the subsequent televised select committee appearance by Lords Hall and Birt, former BBC DG's both, was excoriation by camera. At times it was surreal viewing, like a hybrid revival of *The Thick Of It* and *W1A*. At times it was almost hide behind the sofa stuff as MPs, including several ex-BBC correspondents like the SNP MP John Nicholson forensically ripped into their ennobled ex-bosses and exposed them as either blundering incompetents or liars or even seeking salvation in amnesia. So much so I ducked messages from the BBC asking me for interviews on what I thought of the committee hearing for fear I would lapse into hysterical giggling littered with profanities!

When DGs try playing blame games

Lord Hall, who tried to make great play of being the DG appointed to clear up the Savile scandal, struggled to explain how, given his personal involvement as Head of News in the original Bashir *Panorama* inquiry and the knowledge of the document fakery and the lies involved, the notorious chancer came to be rehired while Hall was DG? Too much going on in too big an organisation for me to get involved didn't wash any more with the MPs than the average licence payer, The absurdity and irresponsibility compounded by Bashir's appointment to the £120, 000 per annum post over cappuccino meetings, without rival candidates being interviewed, topped by the revelation he appeared on screen so infrequently it cost the licence payer £40 grand a pop while he probably earned much more being allowed to moonlight on entertainment gigs for ITV!

I'm not a great fan of Quentin Letts political sketches in *The Times* but couldn't argue with his verdict on Hall's testimony: 'In classic BBC-suit manner, he blamed colleagues. Harding, Munro, Sloman. A couple of Tims. A chap called Steve, now dead. All were artfully dumped upon with phrases such as 'I wasn't going to second guess their judgement' .

Understanding John Birt's bias

'Blame gaming' was Lord Birt's pitch, too, despite being the DG at the time of the original *Panorama* interview and being in that role because of his reputation as the paragon of journalistic rigour and investigatory excellence.

Birt, now 76, also blamed underlings, including his former protégé Hall whom, he said, had failed to alert him to the internal investigation that established Bashir's lies and document fakery. His evidence punctuated conveniently by memory lapses. Like Lord Dyson's inquiry report showing that Hall alerted his boss Birt in April 1996 to Bashir's commissioning of faked documents, initial false denials and his effective decision to forgive the offence and regard Bashir as an 'honest and honourable man'!

Of Bashir, Birt said, 'A very skilled confidence trickster. A crook.' Claiming to have long disliked the 'smell' of him and guilty of 'one of the biggest crimes in the history of broadcasting'

Try explaining that, Lord Birt

True enough, Lord Birt. But that begs the inconvenient question posed by *Private Eye,* in early June 2021 , why, given what he knew back in 1996, Lord Birt's 2002 532-page autobiography listed on page 264 some of the ' brilliant journalists who were brought on' thanks to his leadership of BBC news and current affairs'. Numero uno on his list of bright stars.....er, Martin Bashir. Maybe amnesia set in much earlier after all? I'd never suspected either their Lordships' shared passion for buses...if only as vehicles for throwing other people under.

As Lord Dyson's report noted cryptically: 'Lord Birt has no recollection of commissioning Lord Hall's inquiry, although he accepts he did so', based on reading documents provided to the Dyson inquiry from BBC archives.

In sharp contrast to Birt's damnation of Bashir to MPs, the Dyson report quotes him with much softer appraisal of 'a relatively inexperienced reporter...a foolish young man who has done something daft because he thinks he's replicating what a more experienced person would have done in the circumstances'. Eh?

Don't let Bashir bring down the house

So how much damage has really been done to the BBC's future? For those of us who wouldn't celebrate Bashir bringing down the house, there was some comfort in only 639 complaints being registered in the days after the May 20 publication of Dyson; with *Private Eye* helpfully noting that was less than half the complaints lodged over the local London *Sunday Politics* edition featuring anti-Semitic placards displayed by pro-Palestine demonstrators the same week.

But that doesn't reflect the cacophony of anti-BBC sentiment whipped up on the Wild West of cyberspace and echoed by too many on the Tory right, inside and outside parliament. It was interesting to hear several critical MPs referring to the BBC as a 'state broadcaster' rather than a public service broadcaster. Careless slips of the tongue…or Freudian slips on how they see things to come?

The second half of that question really should terrify all those who genuinely care about independent journalism holding power to account.

About the contributor

Paul Connew is a media commentator/advisor, broadcaster, ex editor of *Sunday Mirror* and deputy editor of the *Daily Mirror,* a former Mirror Group US bureau chief and a (pre-phone hacking era) deputy editor of *The News of the World*, who has worked both for and against the Murdoch empire on both sides of the Atlantic. A columnist with *The New European* and *The Drum.* He comments on media issues for the BBC, Sky News, CNN, Talk Radio, Times Radio, LBC, Al-Jazeera, and Australian Broadcasting. A regular judge of the British Press Awards and the RTS Awards, Connew has been a contributing author for nine previous books in this series.

Chapter 10

The BBC at 100: Rightly under threat?

Robin Aitken was inside the BBC tent as a radio news correspondent. Now he is outside and sees dark forces amassing. Some justified?

As befits a conservative country the British have great reverence for their institutions. This is not blind love – all the nation's institutions, from the Monarchy to the NHS can expect a good public kicking when things go wrong – but generally, after a scandal there are reforms, the dust settles, and the organisation goes stately on its way. This approach to national life owes much to the fact that the United Kingdom is one of the oldest and most stable liberal democracies in the world. This has meant that national institutions are assured of continuity for as long as they prove themselves useful, efficient and popular. For great public bodies the British way has been very much evolution, not revolution.

The senior management of the BBC might take comfort from this but if so they should guard against complacency. These are perilous times for the BBC for two big reasons – one political and one technological. Despite the longevity of many UK institutions dramatic change does sometimes occur (two from recent history: the privatisation of British Rail in 1997 and the closure of the *News of the World* in 2011) and the BBC is not immune. This plain truth was outlined by the newly appointed Director-General, Tim Davie, in his inaugural message to all staff.

"The evidence is unequivocal: the future of a universal BBC can no longer be taken for granted. We have no inalienable right to exist. We are only as good as the value we deliver our audiences, our customers. We must grow that value. That is our simple mission." (September 3 2020)

Framing the argument in terms of consumer value betrays the formative influences in Davie's career: as a former marketing man he sees the problem is terms of delivering value for money. This is very important, but the threats to the BBC's existence come not on grounds of its expense (where a fair-minded comparison shows that it is better value than its commercial, rivals) but from a combination of factors, some outside its control but others which are a consequence of the BBC's own problematical recent history.

Clouds on the horizon: Technological

Taking the technological threat first: the BBC's status as the country's leading cultural institution owes much to its establishment, in the 1920s, as the nation's monopoly broadcaster. The BBC was made the sole provider of radio services partly because of the scarcity of useable wavelengths; that privilege was underpinned by the licence fee – a monopolistic form of financing. Anyone who wanted to listen to the BBC had to buy a licence (for many years set at ten shillings – 50 pence in today's money) and this method of paying for the BBC through taxation has continued ever since. This is accepted by many but – in an age when there is an almost infinite variety of content-providers – it feels like an imposition to those who are dissatisfied with it. What is the justification for a 'national broadcaster' when the internet brings the world into our homes?

The universal licence fee?

There are some people who simply do not like or use the BBC and forcing them to pay presents a problem even seen through the narrow lens of Tim Davie's formulation; the BBC cannot 'grow value' for people who do not want it. As the numbers of these people is growing that has led for calls for the BBC to be made into a subscription service. This is stoutly resisted by the Corporation because the licence-fee underpins its' independence. But therein lies the problem: the BBC is indeed 'independent' and has used that status to develop its own particular world-view. Theoretically, the licence fee, because it is a universal levy, means that the BBC has to listen and represent every point of view; in practice the exact opposite has happened and, cocooned in the certainty of licence-fee revenue, the BBC has seemed to blithely ignored opinion it does not like.

Clouds on the horizon: Editorial

The technological challenge to the BBC is compounded by a calamitous sequence of scandals which have exposed a seeming lack of journalistic integrity at an organisation which makes lofty claims for itself.

On the BBC website(www.bbc.com) under 'Values' the Corporation declares:

"Trust is the foundation of the BBC; we are independent, impartial and honest."

In the light of the BBC's recent history that promise looks unconvincing. At the time of writing (June 2021) the BBC is still processing the aftermath of the Martin Bashir scandal but the past decades have thrown-up a series of episodes casting a dark shadow over the organisation. 2012 was the Corporation's *annus horribilis* when the Jimmy Savile scandal engulfed it. Savile, (who died in 2011) was a BBC DJ and entertainer exposed as a depraved sexual abuser; what was worse was that the BBC had held back on an investigation by *Newsnight* into Savile's crimes. There was a strong suspicion of cover-up. Hard on the heels of that disaster, *Newsnight* managed seriously to libel Lord McAlpine, a former Tory Party treasurer, by labelling *him* a predatory paedophile. These two episodes cost the BBC a large financial settlement as well as the job of the newly-appointed Director-General, George Entwistle. His tenure was just 54 days.

In the years since there have been other problems with BBC journalism some of which attracted headlines – for instance the *Newsnight* presenter Emily Maitlis' anti-Dominic Cummings outburst in May 2020 – but others which have been systemic, rather than individual.

Brexit blues

In this latter category would fall the BBC's coverage of Brexit; over many years according to some research, the BBC consistently got the tone of its coverage wrong. Eurosceptics were rightly convinced that the BBC was irremediably pro-EU; the organisation *News-watch* has methodically monitored BBC output on EU matters over two decades and their results show that there has been, and continues to be, a strong pro-EU bias in the Corporation's journalism. (news-watch.co.uk)

In reaction to this perceived long-term bias, a strong lobby, bitterly opposed to the BBC, has now emerged. This lobby, which comprises Conservative politicians and their supporters, believe that the BBC stands in ideological opposition to them and in recent years they have campaigned against the licence-fee privilege. It is not only Eurosceptics – other critics see the BBC as generally too liberal, too 'woke', too politically correct and are demanding change.

Ominously for the BBC since the December 2019 General Election it has found itself facing a government which sympathises with its critics. The minister responsible for the media, John Whittingdale, said in March 2021 that the BBC could be forced to move to a subscription model when the national roll-out of high-speed broadband was complete (Parliament 1 March 2021 in response to a public petition calling for the licence fee to be scrapped).

The end of the licence fee?

Ending the licence-fee would not in itself mean the end of the BBC, but what it would do is to level the playing field with other broadcasters; the BBC would become just another media business vying for our attention. What is more, because it would have to work harder to attract customers the BBC might be more responsive to the country's mood, less wrapped-up in its own ideological certainties. There is nothing to suggest that the BBC would not be able to cope with a subscription model. One of the underlying factors supporting the BBC's universality is the fact that there is hardly a person in the country who has not, at some time or other, enjoyed at least one of its programmes.

Long-running shows like *'Test Match Special'* or programmes on *Radio Three*, or the smash-hit entertainment show *'Strictly Come Dancing'* have millions of loyal fans and this is the real strength-in-depth of the BBC.

But scandals like the Bashir/Princess Diana interview do real damage to the Corporation's reputation and undermine its credibility. The wrongdoing of Bashir, which was cruel and immoral, was covered-up by senior executives over a period of 25 years according to Lord Dyson's report into the affair. In its wake is impossible now to argue that the BBC is in some way 'special', better and more upright than other media outfits.

The 17th Director-General, Tim Davie, now speaks of the need to reform the organisation because growing numbers no longer trust it to be fair or impartial. The critics are impatient. In 2022 the current Royal Charter under which the BBC operates will be up for mid-term review and it will be no great surprise if the BBC is put on notice that the days of licence fee are numbered. That would represent a great change in the Corporation's status – a real reduction of its privileged status – but given the strength of the BBC 'brand' and the organisation's creative strengths it would not amount to abolition. But it would mean that the BBC would have to work harder to regain the trust of those now disenchanted with it.

Will it make it beyond 100?

Institutional resilience is characteristically British but as it enters its second century the BBC cannot expect to retain a funding mechanism designed in the 1920s; scrapping the licence fee would be challenging but would be the driver of necessary reform in the organisation. After all the scandals and the breaches of its code of impartiality the licence-fee is a comfort blanket the BBC no longer deserves.

About the contributor

Robin Aitken was a BBC reporter for 25 years. He now writes regularly on media matters for the *Daily Telegraph* and a variety of magazines and websites. He lives in Oxford. In 2014 he was awarded an MBE for his work in establishing the Oxford Food Bank (now the Oxford Food Hub).

Chapter 11

Self-created hostages to fortune

The BBC has developed a reputation for arrogantly brushing off criticism and failing to acknowledge and rectify mistakes before the consequent damage to its reputation has been done. Professor Julian Petley suggests some possible reasons for this attitude, and also ways in which the BBC might behave in a less self-destructive manner in future

Speaking on *Channel 4 News*, 20 May 2021, in the wake of the publication of the Dyson Report on the circumstances surrounding Martin Bashir's *Panorama* interview with Princess Diana on 20 November 1995, Lord Grade had some very harsh words for the organisation whose Board of Governors he once chaired: "Their default position always is: 'We're never wrong, we've got it right. We don't care what you say, we don't care what the evidence is, we're right. Now prove us wrong'. And you go through agony getting them to admit something they could have admitted on day one"[10].

On the other hand, once the BBC did finally admit that its handling of the Bashir case had been woeful, it immediately and publicly donned sackcloth and ashes, its own media editor stating that the Report revealed "a catalogue of moral, professional and editorial failures" (Gillett 2020), and *Panorama* and *Newsnight* offering brutally critical assessments of what had gone on in the organisation of which they were a part.

Howls of execration

Inevitably, the Report was the occasion for howls of anti-BBC execration by its numerous enemies in the national press. However, in its contrite response to the Report, the Corporation stood in the starkest possible contrast to the national press, most of whose major players have repeatedly done their utmost to wreck any attempt to improve journalistic standards in their papers. Entirely predictably, however, papers such as the *Mail*, with its twenty pages of anti-BBC bile on 21 May, used the most recent attempt, namely the Leveson Inquiry, to defend themselves as brave defenders of

---

[10] https://www.channel4.com/news/princess-diana-interview-bbcs-cover-up-beyond-belief-says-lord-grade

media freedom and to attack the BBC with considerable venom. Thus, in its Comment column, it raged that the BBC 'sanctimoniously denounces other media organisations at the first hint they may not be squeaky clean … What a hullabaloo the BBC raised when rogue elements [sic] of the red-top Press were accused of phone hacking. The blanket coverage it devoted to that scandal hastened the closure of the *News of the World* and triggered the Leveson Inquiry, with chilling implications for media freedom. Every allegation of dastardly Press practice drew howls of outrage from Television Centre. Today, though, we know the Emperor has no clothes. Behind the sermonising, the broadcaster has been exposed as nothing more than a pious hypocrite. While purporting to be a scourge of dishonesty, it has mirrored the worst excesses of the tabloid journalism it vilifies'

Media frenzy around Diana

But not everything that appears in the *Mail* is wrong by definition, and that last sentence may just contain a grain of truth. (It also needs to be remembered that, whatever its motive, it was the *Mail on Sunday* that first drew attention to the 'Bashir problem', and as early as April 1996). It has to be borne in mind that the interview happened when there was a media frenzy of gigantic proportions around Princess Diana.

The main instigators of this frenzy, which ultimately led to her death, were, of course, British national newspapers, which renders their recent accusations that Bashir and the BBC were "hounding" her more than usually hypocritical and two-faced. In such a hyper-competitive media environment, Bashir's use of subterfuge to obtain the interview, and the BBC hierarchy's unwillingness to admit that he had done so, perhaps become more understandable, whilst of course remaining wholly unacceptable and indeed reprehensible.

The wider media landscape in which the BBC operates also needs to be borne in mind when examining a more recent story, namely the televised police raid on Sir Cliff Richard's home, when, in pursuit of a tabloid-style scandal, the BBC made a number of very serious editorial misjudgements, refused to back down in the face of threats of legal action, and then found itself fighting a case it was almost bound to lose, which indeed it did.

'Breathless sensationalism'

In 2014, Dan Johnson, a north-of-England correspondent for BBC News, discovered that South Yorkshire Police (SYP) were investigating the singer Sir Cliff Richard who, it had been alleged anonymously, had abused a thirteen-year-old 30 years ago.

Johnson and SYP then entered into a highly controversial arrangement whereby they would inform him when Richard's Sunningdale home was to be searched. This happened on 14 August, and the BBC hired a helicopter from which to film the raid. Johnson and a BBC crew were also sent to camp outside the gates.

The BBC decided to broadcast the story on the *One O'Clock News*, but, in order to scoop rival outlets, did so without seeking a response from the singer. The decision was signed off by Fran Unsworth, then deputy to Director of News James Harding.

No arrests were made and Richard was never charged, but the BBC refused to apologise and insisted that it had run a story that was in the public interest. Meanwhile the SYP settled out of court. Richard offered not to sue the BBC if it agreed to make a public apology, but its Director-General, Tony Hall, refused. The case came to court in 2018 and Richard won £210,000 in damages after Mr Justice Mann ruled that the BBC had seriously violated his privacy and had done so "with a significant degree of breathless sensationalism"[11]. He was awarded a further £20,000 in aggravated damages for the Corporation's decision to nominate its story for the Royal Television Society's 'scoop of the year' award. The BBC spent £1.9m in legal costs.

'A reasonable expectation of privacy'

English laws on contempt ban the media from publishing information that might seriously prejudice active legal proceedings, which means that news coverage of a case is limited once an individual is charged. But Mr Justice Mann argued that "a suspect has a reasonable expectation of privacy in relation to a police investigation", raising concerns among many news outlets that the judgement severely limited the media's ability to report the fact that an individual is under investigation by the police before any charges have actually been brought.

Indeed, immediately after the judgement this very claim was made by Fran Unsworth, who stated that it created "new case law" and "represents a dramatic shift against press freedom and the long-standing ability of journalists to report on police investigations" (quoted in Mayhew 2018). Such concerns were echoed across the press (see, for example, Waterson 2018a; Tobitt 2018; Greenslade 2018).

---

[11] The full judgement can be found at https://www.judiciary.uk/wp-content/uploads/2018/07/cliff-richard-v-bbc-judgment.pdf

Mr Justice Mann acknowledged that his judgment was "capable of having a significant impact on press reporting" but insisted that he was not changing or extending the law but merely balancing the right to privacy and the right to freedom of expression in line with the requirements of the Human Rights Act 1998 and subsequent privacy judgements.

The public interest

In this respect the judge made it abundantly clear that the right to privacy could be over-ridden if the public interest required it in a specific case, but that in *this* particular case there was absolutely no such interest in revealing Richard's identity. Cutting straight through the press hysteria and misinformation, David Elstein (2018) explained that,

'without any public interest, the BBC's decision to name Cliff Richard at all – never mind the helicopter hired to film the search of his flat, and the huge prominence given to the story – was "an invasion of Sir Cliff's privacy rights in a big way", made despite the BBC knowing well in advance that the police had decided not to publicise a name ... The BBC tried to argue that investigations of historic sex offences were a subject of significant public interest which ought to be reported: and the judge agreed that the *fact* of an investigation might be a matter of public interest; but naming the target required a much higher level of significance, and in this case amounted to no more, in his view, than the BBC encouraging gossip-mongers in its pursuit of scoops and headlines'.

As Mr Justice Mann himself put it: "I do not believe that this [public interest] justification was much in the minds of those at the BBC at the time. I think that they, or most of them, were far more impressed by the size of the story and that they had the opportunity to scoop their rivals".

Johnson hunting 'celebrity paedos'

As the court's judgement makes abundantly clear, the very *manner* in which the BBC covered the story compounded the damage done to Richard's privacy. Mr Justice Mann noted that Gary Smith, the BBC UK News Editor, was "obsessed with the merits of scooping news rivals", whilst Johnson "was capable of letting his enthusiasm get the better of him in pursuit of what he thought was a good story".

And the court heard that Johnson, in true tabloid style, had e-mailed colleagues that he was investigating "celebrity paedos" (quoted in Waterson 2018b). Mr Justice Mann stressed that he was awarding Richard far higher damages (£190,000) than those awarded to Max Mosley

(£60,000) in his privacy action case against the *News of the World* because the invasion of privacy here was at least "twice as bad", not least because of the world-wide publicity resulting from the dozens of news reports the BBC had broadcast, with great fanfare and huge prominence for the story on its bulletins.

He concluded that "this was a very serious invasion of privacy rights, which had a very adverse effect". Similar considerations lay behind the award for aggravated damages on account of the RTS nomination, the judge arguing that in promoting "its own [privacy] infringing activity in a way which demonstrates that it is extremely proud of it", the BBC had caused Richard additional distress "both by demonstrating its pride and unrepentance and to a degree repeating the invasion of privacy with a metaphorical fanfare".

What human rights?

One of the most extraordinary aspects of the Cliff Richard affair is that, when discussing coverage of the police raid, senior BBC staff such as Unsworth appear not to have taken into account the matter of Richard's human rights. Tabloid newspapers are notorious for their hatred of the Human Rights Act 1998, which they perceive – entirely correctly – as curbing their worst privacy-busting excesses, but the BBC's actions seem to have been governed more by ignorance of human rights jurisprudence. As Mr Justice Mann noted: "The principal concern of the BBC seems to have been factual accuracy and defamation, and not privacy-related concerns. Apparently the lawyers had not flagged that up to her [Unsworth] as a specific risk". Furthermore, during the case itself, the BBC claimed that a privacy suit could not include compensation for reputational damage, as this was the province of defamation law. However, the judge strongly disagreed arguing that:

'Reputational harm can arise from matters of fact which are true but within the scope of a privacy right .... If the protection of reputation is part of the function of privacy law then that must be reflected in the right of the court to give damages which relate to loss of reputation ....The facts of this case (on the footing that the public interest in reporting does not outweigh Sir Cliff's privacy rights) vividly demonstrate why damages should be available for an invasion of privacy resulting (inter alia) in damage to reputation'.

'We overdid it'

Eight days after the conclusion of the case, the BBC applied to Mr Justice Mann for permission to appeal, which he rejected. The BBC considered approaching the Court of Appeal directly, but then decided against it on the grounds that it would be extremely expensive, that there was no realistic chance of overturning the judgement and that it risked a public backlash if it went ahead (public opinion was firmly on Cliff Richard's side). Tony Hall told the DCMS select committee: "I felt the case itself was not one I was happy to go to appeal on because of the way I thought we overdid it" (quoted in Davies 2018).

The temptation of tabloidisation

Much has recently, albeit very belatedly, been written about the BBC increasingly shadowing the political agenda of the predominantly right-wing daily press. But what I have attempted to explore here are a number of other issues which arise for the BBC as a result of working in a journalistic environment dominated by newspapers whose values are not only different from but antithetical to those of public service broadcasting. most obvious of these issues is the temptation of tabloidization. The effects of this process inside the BBC have been illuminatingly discussed by Corporation veteran Kevin Marsh, who notes that "around the turn the century, a new strand of thinking gained traction at the top of the BBC. The idea that we were too cautious. That we didn't break enough stories and weren't taking on the press as aggressively as we should" (2012: 81).

Such an idea was supported by the new Director-General, Greg Dyke, and also by Rod Liddle, then editor at *Today* from 1998 to 2002.The latter argued that the BBC should be doing more original, "exclusive" journalism and that "in order to deliver it, *Today*, needed to import some of the thinking, and some of the people, from what we used to call Fleet Street The idea of a more tabloid agenda, 'breaking more stories', appealed to Liddle" (ibid.: 81-2). One of the "imports", notoriously, was Andrew Gilligan, formerly of the *Sunday Telegraph*, whose story on 29 May 2003 alleging that the government had 'sexed up' a dossier about Saddam Hussein's possession of weapons of mass destruction was to lead to the Hutton Inquiry and the resignation of both Dyke and the BBC's chairman Gavyn Davies. At the Inquiry an e-mail emerged from Kevin Marsh, who had taken over from Liddle at *Today*, to Stephen Mitchell, Head of Radio News, in which he stated that 'this story was a good piece of investigative journalism, marred by flawed reporting – our biggest millstone has been his loose use of language and lack of judgment in some of his phraseology'. However, the BBC insisted on defending Gilligan's report, and Marsh's reservations were ignored.

Choosing the right battles

One of the paradoxes here, of course, is that press which the BBC sometimes seems so keen to ape is also the Corporation's sworn enemy. But perhaps if the BBC competed less with newspapers on their own terms, they might regard it as less of a rival and moderate their hostility somewhat. On the other hand, the reasons for their hatred are as much political and ideological as economic, so this might not make an appreciable difference.

But whatever the case, it must be extraordinarily galling for the BBC to be the daily target of vituperation from newspapers whose own journalistic standards are so shockingly low, and this may tempt the BBC into failing to respond to valid criticisms from this quarter, or indeed to digging in over-defensively when such criticisms are made – thus contributing to the situation outlined by Lord Grade at the start of this chapter.

In my view, the BBC actually needs to be far more combative when it comes to dealing with the press – but it also needs to choose it battles very carefully and, above all, to avoid offering hostages to fortune of the kind discussed in this chapter.

About the contributor

Julian Petley is emeritus and honorary professor of journalism at Brunel University London His most recent book is the second edition of *Culture Wars: The Media and the British Left* (Routledge 2019), co-written with James Curran and Ivor Gaber. He is a member of the editorial board of the *British Journalism Review* and the principal editor of the *Journal of British Cinema and Television*. A former print journalist, he now contributes to online publications such as *Inforrm*, *Byline Times* and *openDemocracy*.

References

Davies, Caroline (2018) 'BBC coverage of Cliff Richard raid was over the top, says Tony Hall', *Guardian*, 11 September. Available online at
https://www.theguardian.com/media/2018/sep/11/bbc-to-cut-back-online-services-to-fight-netflix-say-reports

Elstein, David (2018) 'The BBC and Cliff Richard: what threat to press liberty?', openDemocracy, 27 July. Available at https://www.opendemocracy.net/en/ourbeeb/bbc-and-cliff-richard-what-threat-to-press-liberty/

Gillett, Francesca (2020) 'Martin Bashir: inquiry criticises BBC over "deceitful" Diana interview', BBC News, 20 May. Available online at https://www.bbc.co.uk/news/uk-57189371

Greenslade, Roy (2018), 'The Cliff Richard ruling is a chilling blow to press freedom', Guardian, 18 July. Available online at https://www.theguardian.com/commentisfree/2018/jul/18/cliff-richard-bbc-press-freedom-privacy

Marsh, Kevin (2012) Stumbling over Truth: The Inside Story of the 'Sexed Up' Dossier, Hutton and the BBC, London: Biteback Publishing.

Mayhew, Freddy (2018) 'BBC News director says Sir Cliff ruling marks "dramatic shift against press freedom" as Society of Editors calls High Court judgement "worrying"', Press Gazette, 18 July. Available online at https://www.pressgazette.co.uk/bbc-news-director-says-sir-cliff-ruling-marks-dramatic-shift-against-press-freedom-as-society-of-editors-calls-high-court-judgement-worrying/

Tobitt, Charlotte (2018) 'Newspapers back BBC over Sir Cliff Privacy ruling creating "new right to anonymity" for police suspects in "dark day for journalism"', Press Gazette, 19 July. Available online at https://www.pressgazette.co.uk/newspapers-back-bbc-over-sir-cliff-privacy-ruling-creating-new-right-to-anonymity-for-police-suspects-in-dark-day-for-journalism/

Waterson, Jim (2018a) 'Media experts alarmed at consequences of Cliff Richard ruling', Guardian, 18 July. Available online at https://www.theguardian.com/music/2018/jul/18/media-experts-alarmed-at-consequences-of-cliff-richard-ruling

Waterson, Jim (2018b) 'BBC reporter "guessed" Cliff Richard was subject of sexual assault allegation', Guardian, 18 April. Available online at https://www.theguardian.com/music/2018/apr/18/bbc-reporter-guessed-cliff-richard-was-subject-of-sexual-assault-investigation

Chapter 12

The BBC and the end of the 'good chap' culture

We need a strong BBC in the era of fake news and fake norms, but the BBC must ensure its processes are above criticism to play the role that is needed, which makes its response to Dyson absolutely critical. Professor Leighton Andrews, formerly Head of Public Affairs at the BBC

1995 wasn't only the year of the BBC's Diana interview. Lord Nolan's Committee on Standards in Public Life reported that year, establishing seven standards which remain recognised and recommended today: selflessness; integrity; objectivity; accountability; openness; honesty; leadership. Meanwhile, the journalist and historian Peter Hennessy published his book on the unacknowledged operations behind the UK's unwritten constitution, *The Hidden Wiring,* which popularised the notion of 'the good chap' theory of government:

A good chap knows what a good chap is expected to do and will never push things too far (Hennessy, 1995: 57).

Hennessy had little to say about the BBC's role in the UK's *secret* unwritten constitution, but as we look back now at the Bashir business we can see the deep entanglement of the BBC and other institutions said to define Britishness – such as the Royal Family – exposed for all to see.

For the BBC may be a broadcaster, a programme-maker, a news operation, a collection of diverse media services, a series of small and medium-sized cultural enterprises with – in theory – a binding culture of excellence. But it is above all an institution. And it is an institution shaped and constructed by internal and external forces and an institution heavily involved in the shaping of the cultures of the nations of the UK and also the British state.

The BBC and Buck House

The Diana interview had immediate repercussions for the BBC's relationship with the Royal Family, confirmed in emails subsequently released under Freedom of Information (Hastings, 2006). The Royal Family – and individual senior royals – have a sophisticated media operation, and the BBC was on the receiving end of it for years afterwards.

For some time in 2020, Charles Moore was being touted as a possible chair of the BBC. Moore himself, as he has admitted, was something of a player in the events around the Diana interview:

'When [the BBC] announced, six days before the broadcast, that the interview had taken place, I telephoned Hussey to ask what was going on. He informed me that he had been told nothing, and said he was outraged' (Moore, C. 2021a).

Moore was Hussey's outlet for some time afterwards:

'The interview aired. Not long afterwards, I spoke to Hussey again. He told me he was trying to persuade his board to condemn the BBC's methods, but of course it was too late. He left the BBC within a few months' (Moore, C. 2021a).

That there were tensions between the BBC Board of Management and BBC Governors at this time is now well-known, and was confirmed recently by John Birt when he gave evidence to the Commons Digital, Culture, Media and Sport committee in June 2021:

'I had had an excellent relationship with the Chairman of the BBC over the best part of 10 years but it had deteriorated over the previous year' (House of Commons, 2021).

Birt decided to tell Hussey after the interview was recorded but a week before transmission.

As an ex-editor, Moore has expressed a 'sneaking sympathy' with BBC leaders in wanting to get the interview on screen (Moore, C. 2021b). But he makes the argument, which in the context of the BBC's governance structure at the time, is not an unfair one, that it was for Hussey to decide whether he was conflicted, not for BBC management to do so (Moore, 2021a). However, John Birt, who agonised over when to tell Hussey and was clear that he felt he might be putting his own job on the line, reminded the Commons Committee that the BBC owed a duty to its interviewee:

'I had to make a decision. Princess Diana only imposed one condition, which was that she and only she should inform the Queen when the interview was done' (House of Commons, 2021).

Who governed the BBC?

The split between the two BBC boards provoked the possibility of such clashes. The BBC governance system itself at the time was evidence of the 'good chap' culture in action. But as the government has acknowledged, the BBC governance system has changed twice since then.

No-one now doubts that Martin Bashir's activities were dodgy or that he was a serial liar. The BBC's decision to re-hire him in 2016 was not, says the MacQuarrie report (2021), part of a plot to encourage him to stay silent. But the re-hiring certainly comes close to what has been called 'wilful blindness' (Heffernan, 2012), and as Kevin Brennan MP said in his questioning at the parliamentary hearing, the BBC's employment practices in the Bashir case reeked of 'chumocracy'.

Lord Dyson says (2021:4) that it was likely that, even without Bashir's forgeries, Princess Diana would have granted an interview to someone. Experienced women journalists have rightly said (Long, 2021; Moore, S. 2021) that too much of the post-Dyson commentary has looked like attempts to deny Diana her own agency in deciding to do the interview.

Blackballing Bashir/News mis-information

One aspect of the 'good chap' culture has had little coverage, aside from an article in *The Times* (Low, 2021), reporting comments of Earl Spencer:

'At some point, he said, there was talk of Bashir getting a role as a leading presenter with the BBC. Spencer said he spoke to his brother-in-law Robert Fellowes — Lord Fellowes, who was then the Queen's private secretary — about it. "Robert had a word with the BBC and that was the end."

As former BBC News Weekly Programmes Managing Editor David Aaronovitch tweeted:

'Assuming that this account of the interview is correct and that Spencer was correct in what he said, it would be a massive capitulation by the BBC to outside pressure'. (Aaronovitch, 2021)

Aaronovitch said he thought it inconceivable that the BBC would have bowed to such pressure. But that, of course, was how the 'good chap' culture worked: private, unrecordable chats and actions taken on the basis of them.

One issue reported by Lord Dyson but ignored in the parliamentary scrutiny was the fact that a BBC Publicity Officer Alison Jackson (now Kelly) was asked to brief the media that stories about fake bank statements were being leaked by 'jealous colleagues' of Bashir on *Panorama*. Lord Dyson records:

'I am certain that the account given to me by Mrs Kelly was true…. It is clear that someone at the BBC instructed her to give this briefing to the press. The material that I have seen and heard does not enable me to identify that person' (Dyson, 2021: 85).

It is clear that experienced BBC journalists with concerns about Bashir were being briefed against externally. The Dyson report also suggests that they were being warned off internally.

Institutions run blame avoidance strategies (Hood, 2011). It looks like *Panorama* whistle-blowers were thrown under the bus of institutional blame avoidance. As Tony Hall told MPs, following the inquiries into the Jimmy Savile scandals, he oversaw a revamping of BBC whistle-blowing procedures in 2015 (House of Commons, 2021; BBC, 2015). Would that have protected whistle-blowers in 1995 or 1996? It would certainly have given them reassurance.

Trust and losing it

Why does this matter so much today? After all, it was 25 years ago. It matters, because the BBC depends on trust – the trust of its audiences, the trust that senior managers have in programme-makers and managers throughout the system, and vice versa, and the trust that governments and parliamentarians place in the BBC's governance and management. Fortunately, the BBC, following a period of Beeb-bashing in early 2020, demonstrated its value during the pandemic and emerged as a crucial part of the UK and devolved government response (Andrews, 2020, 2021). The UK Government has signalled that it will give the BBC space to develop its own proposals for reform.

We live in an era not just of fake news, but of fake norms. The Nolan rules became secondary to the pursuit of Brexit. The process of their undermining began when Theresa May was Prime Minister, but has accelerated since Johnson took over in 2019, with the Ministerial Code's foreword placing the pursuit of Brexit at its heart. Everything else is subservient to that (Andrews, 2019), and Covid of course has provided further opportunities for the avoidance of what Dominic Cummings has called 'Potemkin' processes (Vaughan, 2021)

What we are left with is the reality of state power in the hands of people whose routine justification is the realpolitik of the people's will. A strong, impartial and independent BBC is sorely needed. At the Commons hearing in June 2021, one MP suggested that the current Prime Minister had been sacked from a newspaper (naming the wrong one, in fact) for doing less than Bashir got away with. That shows how exposed the BBC is on issues of honesty, trust and impartiality.

The era of the good chaps is over, and the BBC needs to be better than them and squeaky-clean.

About the contributor

Leighton Andrews is Professor in Public Service Leadership at Cardiff Business School. He was formerly Minister for Education and Minister for Public Services in the Welsh Governments from 2009-16. He was the BBC's Head of Public Affairs from 1993-1996.His most recent book is *Facebook, the Media and Democracy,* (Routledge, 2019). Recent publications include articles on the BBC and European media policymaking in *International Journal of Cultural Policy* and on the Nolan Rules in *Political Quarterly*

References

Aaronovitch, D. 2021. Twitter Feed, 22 May, https://mobile.twitter.com/daaronovitch/status/1396064850795810821

Andrews, L. 2019. Brexit, Cabinet Norms and the Ministerial Code: are we living in a post-Nolan Era? Political Quarterly, vol 19 (1). 125-133. https://doi.org/10.1111/1467-923X.12778

Andrews, L. 2020. The BBC – Broadcasting, Britishness, and the Culture Wars, in John Mair (Ed). The BBC: A Winter of Discontent? Goring: Bite-sized Books.

Andrews, L. 2021 (In Press). 'Like any wartime government': Covid-19, Churchillian Imaginaries, English exceptionalism and the battle of Britishness, In Jo Pettit (ed). Covid-19, WW2, and the idea of Britishness, Oxford: Peter Lang Publishing.

BBC, 2015. Review of the BBC Whistleblowing and Child Protection Policies and Processes, BBC Executive, July. http://downloads.bbc.co.uk/aboutthebbc/insidethebbc/howwework/reports/pdf/goodcorporation_bbc_whistleblowing_childprotectionpolicies_processes.pdf

Dyson, L. 2021. Report of the Dyson Investigation. BBC, 20 May. http://downloads.bbc.co.uk/aboutthebbc/reports/reports/dyson-report-20-may-21.pdf

Hastings, C. 2006 Queen sacked us over Diana interview, says BBC, Daily Telegraph, 29 January. https://www.telegraph.co.uk/news/1509088/Queen-sacked-us-over-Diana-interview-says-BBC.html

Heffernan, M. 2012. Wilful Blindness: why we ignore the obvious at our peril. London: Simon and Schuster.

Hennessy, P. 1995. The Hidden Wiring, London: Victor Gollancz.

Hood, C. 2011. The Blame Game. Princeton: Princeton University Press.

House of Commons, 2021. Digital, Culture, Media and Sport Committee, Oral Evidence: The Work of the BBC, HC 257, 15 June. https://committees.parliament.uk/oralevidence/2350/pdf/

Long, C. 2021.Even now, Diana is not allowed to tell us she wanted to do that interview, Sunday Times, 23 May. https://www.thetimes.co.uk/article/even-now-diana-is-not-allowed-to-tell-us-she-wanted-to-do-that-interview-3b2vvc0zg

Low, V. 2021. Earl Spencer believed palace flat was bugged to dupe Diana, The Times, 22 May. https://www.thetimes.co.uk/article/earl-spencer-believed-palace-flat-was-bugged-to-dupe-diana-bhtkb879t

MacQuarrie, K. 2021 A review to establish the facts around the decision by the BBC to appoint Martin Bashir as Religious Affairs Correspondent in September 2016 and the subsequent re-grading of the role to Religion Editor in 2018. BBC, 14 June. http://downloads.bbc.co.uk/aboutthebbc/reports/reports/martin-bashir-appointment-review.pdf

Moore, C. 2021a. Prince William is right about the BBC: public service broadcasting and fake news can't mix, Daily Telegraph, 21 May. https://www.telegraph.co.uk/news/2021/05/21/prince-william-right-bbc-public-service-broadcasting-fake-news/

Moore, C. 2021b Why the BBC believed Martin Bashir, Spectator 19 June, https://www.spectator.co.uk/article/why-the-bbc-believed-martin-bashir

Moore, S. 2021. Diana. Defund the Monarchy. Letters from Suzanne, 21 May. https://suzannemoore.substack.com/p/diana-defund-the-monarchy?r=cldek&utm_campaign=post&utm_medium=web&utm_source=twitter

Vaughan, R. 2021. Dominic Cummings defends appointment of Public First after High Court 'unlawful' ruling. The i, 9 June https://inews.co.uk/news/politics/dominic-cummings-defends-appointment-public-first-high-court-unlawful-ruling-1042933

Section three
Current Affairs and Tomorrow's BBC World

Introduction

John Mair

The BBC is in a seeming perma-crisis. The enemies are circling the wagons ready for the publication of Minister John Whittingdale's Public Service Review and the BBC Charter Review in 2022.Like the cover of this book, the storm clouds are gathering. How does the BBC dig itself out of the many elephant traps existentially threatening it?

This section attempts to provide some answers. First up Marcus Ryder, recognised for his sterling work in 'decolonising' British broadcasting, in *Communities: The unloved third child in the BBC Charter* says it should accept the realities of Britain in 2021-Diverse in many ways, A collection of communities.

'The BBC has survived, and even thrived, over the last 100 years because it has recognised the importance of reflecting how society and its audience view themselves. Without an organisational structure that prioritises the UK's diverse communities it is failing to do this'.

One huge community with whom the Corporation has had to make its peace is the half of the population that are women, In *The BBC's woman problem* Fiona Chesterton,who rose to become one of the more senior woman in the BBC and Channel Four, looks to a future beyond macho management a quarter of a century ago-and now?

'Reading Lord Dyson's report on what happened in 1995 and the following year when suspicion fell on the methods used by this now notorious *Panorama* reporter to obtain the interview with Princess Diana, I felt an overpowering whiff of testosterone arising from its pages. With one exception, all the senior managers at the BBC at the time who had a role in investigating the affair internally were male. Nearly all were men who I would describe as 'clubbable', ambitious, well-schooled in the arts of corporate P.R and, perhaps, prone to confusing the interests of the BBC – and even their own personal ones -with the public interest. '

Complaints about their complaints system are an eternal thorn in the side of the Corporation. It may, but only may be resolving that after a century. In

No More Marking their own homework: The BBC and audience complaints. Professor Ivor Gaber recalls his experiences as the complained against whilst a programme maker and the BBC Trust referee for complaints. Neither was satisfactory. He thinks *Ofcom* may be the answer.

Moving to the future and the seeming unstoppable rise in the UK and globally of the 'California Streamers-*Netflix, Amazon Prime, Apple and Disney +*, Bernard Clark-TV reporter turned media mogul- in *The BBC is 100. Hurrah! Long live the BBC?* blames the government and BBC timidity for losing the electronic Crown Jewels. The authorities put *Project Kangaroo*, which would have captured the streaming market for the UK a decade ago, firmly back into its perch. It simply shot the baby animal on competition grounds. Others took over the territory with huge success. There oligopoly is there for all to see. The BBC does not escape Clark's excoriation.

'I think of the BBC as full of villains, yes villains. From the members of the Executive Committee down to middle management, they are weak, indecisive, compliant figures who have been shoe-horned into supervisory roles, and stand up neither to Government, nor the life-timers inside the BBC.'

Peter York, the social commentator turned General of the BBC Defenders Army, if of a different world view. In *Netflix is not the BBC* he attempts to put clear blue water between the public purposes of the corporation and the US Video on demand providers

'when someone confused tells you we don't need the BBC now we've got the lovely new 'California Streamers', or that the BBC is full of woke moaners or crazed communists just ask them a few simple questions. If the world has another pandemic, a catastrophic recession or seems to be limbering up for WW3, who you gonna call, the BBC – or a Disney cartoon princess?' Ouch.

Steve Clarke observes the BBC monthly as editor of the RTS magazine *'Television'*. He is very passionate about one special part of the output-Arts- and sees the Corporation failing there. In *The arts of the possible* he says they need to get better on programming in that genre , where they are being outshone by *Sky Arts* and even *Netflix* longer term and not just for tactical reasons

'The cynical view is that the BBC only every really ups its cultural game when Charter Renewal beckons. The present Charter is guaranteed until December 31, 2027. That doesn't mean that Tim Davie should risk diluting the loyalty of those licence fee payers who want and expect a rich and varied diet across the arts on radio, TV and online'.

For some, The BBC was the playground of the white upper class. The one nationalised industry they supported. One long party. David Lancaster has had four decades both attending the feast inside the BBC and later teaching about it. In *Is the party over?* this hackademic from the University of Leeds mulls over the warm white wine of the BBC office Xmas party and looks back to halcyon days where Public Service broadcasting was easily defined.

'In the case of the BBC I knew, the term meant, in essence, anything the Corporation cared to do, whether it was blatantly populist, or relatively esoteric. This confusion was inherent in the very way the institution was constructed (or cobbled together). The overriding principle was to justify what the neo-liberals would later call the "poll tax" of the licence fee'

Finally in this section Dr Liam McCarthy, a BBC local radio manager turned scholar, thinks the way forward is rebuilding the local roots of the Corporation. In *Levelling up: Making the BBC personally relevant again* he puts the case. The BBC was stymied in its attempt to provide uber local news using the internet a decade ago by the frantic lobbying of the local press. That succeeded, the project died but they have failed, Now more than ever a local BBC is needed due to the long slow death of the local papers and the rapid consolidation of local commercial TV and radio broadcasting. As he puts it' There is a market failure in local print and commercial radio journalism and a growing democratic deficit in which politicians and local leaders are not being held to account. Media consolidation in the UK has resulted in four out of five newspapers and four out of five commercial local radio companies being owned by just seven companies'

The roads out of the perma-crisis and a future are many and varied for the BBC as it enters its second century. The hope is that the rabid 'whack-a-mole' populism of the Johnson government does not lead it down a blind alley with no end in 2022.

Chapter 13

Communities: The unloved third child in the BBC Charter

Marcus Ryder, formerly a senior BBC editor, reflects on a job for which he did not apply and for which he might in the future – if and only if – the job description changes

"I want to be Head of BBC Diversity"

I was talking informally to a very senior executive of the corporation over a coffee in a restaurant just off Carnaby Street in London a few years ago.

The executive's response was direct and to the point.

"Why on earth do you want to do that Marcus?" The exec took a sip of their drink and explained their thinking by way of a compliment, "I see you as having a really bright future at the Beeb. You are one of the few Black people with news and current affairs experience at an executive producer level, you've overseen some really complicated investigations, and you've had to make some really tough Political calls in Scotland."

Then came the killer punch.

"Head of Diversity will take you away from all of that – it will lead your career up a blind alley. It's not where you want to be, if you want real power."

I have no delusions of grandeur regarding my career in British broadcasting in general, and the BBC in particular, but I had heard his argument before and given it some thought.

I responded with what I felt at the time was a power move:

"I guess you and I see diversity slightly differently," I replied. "Think of it this way; Kenny (I was referring to Ken MacQuarrie) is a major player on the BBC's executive board as Director of BBC Scotland. He is effectively in charge of one of the most important parts of the BBC – and overseeing over a thousand members of staff and millions of pounds worth of programming budget.

"I don't want to be Head of Diversity if it's just as an extension of Human Resources, or Head of Diversity simply advising on how to get a few more Black people or women on screen, or even behind it. I want to be Head of Diversity at the BBC in the same way Kenny is head of Scotland – with real power.

"The BBC needs to restructure – it is not only vital for media diversity, it is essential for the corporation's survival".

My power move that day was unnecessary.

Restructuring the job, widening the core

Needless to say, I did not become Head of Diversity, and although the BBC did go on to raise both the profile and position of the Head of Diversity role it did not restructure in the way I believed was so vital.

That said, I still believe that restructuring is necessary. To understand why, we first have to understand the BBC's current structure and charter.

The BBC's Charter in 2007 states that one of the core purposes of the corporation is to represent "the UK, its nations, regions and communities".

But this is not new. The BBC has always recognised the importance of representing the UK's different Nations and the Regions. The 1952 Charter formalised the idea of National Broadcasting Councils and Regional Advisory Councils. These represented the interests and culture of Scotland, England, Wales, Northern Ireland and different geographic regions both in terms of output and in the running of the corporation.

The importance of the Nations and Regions is seen as so intrinsic to the structure of the BBC that Ken MacQuarrie (then Head of BBC Scotland whom I spoke about earlier) who was later promoted to Head of Nations and Regions, described the role he left in 2020 as "one of the BBC's largest and most high profile divisions".

Then, when Rhodri Talfan Davies took over from MacQuarrie in December 2020, the BBC Director General said Davies "brings considerable *editorial* and strategic experience [to the role]" (my italics). Note the word "*editorial*".

This was precisely the quality that the senior BBC executive in the restaurant told me the BBC Head of Diversity lacked, and why they saw it as a "dead-end" for my career.

What's missing from the job description?

Now if you hadn't noticed it already, let me point out the glaring omission from Ken MacQuarrie and Rhodri Talfan Davies' job titles. Despite the BBC Charter explicitly highlighting the importance of the UK's "nations, regions and *communities*", the job which is meant to be specifically in charge of ensuring this, only includes two out of these three areas: the nations and regions.

Despite it being written into the charter since 1952 there is (still) no one explicitly responsible in the BBC for the UK's communities.

Many people working in the field of diversity and inclusion have previously seen reference to "communities" in the charter to implicitly refer to diversity.

In 2017, after campaigning and lobbying by Sir Lenny Henry, myself and others this implicit understanding was made explicit when the Charter was updated to include the principle of "diversity", stating one of the corporation's core public purposes is, "to reflect, represent and serve the *diverse* communities of all of the United Kingdom's nations and regions" (my italics).

While the BBC Charter correctly identifies diverse communities on par with the nations and regions, the corporation seems to have consistently overlooked them. Diversity at the BBC is fundamentally framed as either an HR problem, or one of influencing the creativity of the corporation. People working in diversity have little or no editorial power, and importantly there is no diversity role on the BBC's News board. Yet, no one would ever suggest taking this approach to how the BBC oversees the nations and regions.

This is a mistake.

Accept the reality of Britain in 2021

The reality is that in 2021 the UK's diverse communities are increasingly and possibly as important to British people's identities than their nationality (English, Scottish, Welsh or Northern Irish) or in which geographical region they live.

While the BBC's structure embedding the importance of the nations and regions, while overlooking communities, might have made sense 15 or even over 50 years ago, it looks increasingly arcane and out of touch with the needs of a modern public service broadcaster in the UK.

The fact is, Britain is a fundamentally different society to the one it was when the BBC was born, in a multitude of ways.

Let's look at this chronologically.

In 1971 the UK census recorded ethnicity for the first time. That year, the White population made up roughly 97.7 percent of the population. According to the 2011 census the non-White population in the UK is 13 per cent, and the 2021 census is expected to show that it has grown even larger.

In 1980, homosexual acts in private between two men in private were finally de-criminalised in Scotland, despite the Sexual Offences Bill 1967 de-criminalising homosexual acts between two men in England and Wales.

It took until 1995 for the many of the rights we now take for granted of disabled people to be recognised in the UK under the Disability Discrimination Act.

Put simply, how Britain now formally recognises these different communities both in terms of law, and in general public discourse has undergone a rapid transformation over the last fifty years.

Yet, the BBC structures still places communities as an afterthought at best, and completely ignores them at worst.

The BBC has survived, and even thrived, over the last 100 years because it has recognised the importance of reflecting how society and its audience view themselves. Without an organisational structure that prioritises the UK's diverse communities it is failing to do this.

This is not just my assertion. An *Ofcom* report in 2018 suggested that many communities in the UK are increasingly dissatisfied with the broadcaster and simply switching off. While another report, Mind the Viewing Gap, in 2015 by digital.i showed that non-White people made up only 6 per cent of PSB viewing despite making up 14 per cent of the population.

Reflecting on my conversation that day in the restaurant with the senior BBC executive I think I made just one mistake. I do not want to be head of BBC Diversity.

I want to be Head of BBC Diverse Communities. And when the BBC creates the position – which I believe it will have to one day in order to survive – I hope I will be just about young enough to send in my CV.

About the contributor

Marcus Ryder is the Head of External Consultancies at the Sir Lenny Henry Centre for Media Diversity and the Chair of Council for RADA (Royal Academy of Dramatic Arts). He was the head of current affairs programming for BBC Scotland from 2007 – 2015.

Chapter 14

The BBC's woman problem

Fiona Chesterton argues that a bigger scandal than the BBC's well publicised issues with the gender pay gap, is about power, not money. In the Corporation's first 100 years, there has been a power gap – with not a single woman becoming Director-General.

In 2019 I wrote an open letter to what I imagined would be the first female Director-General of the BBC (*Is the BBC in Peril* ed. Mair and Bradshaw, pub Bite-Sized Books 2020). How foolish and naïve of me! Later that year, the seventeenth DG was appointed, and yes, he was a man, Tim Davie, of course.

A few months after that, amid speculation that the Government might appoint a suitably Conservative-friendly woman to chair the board, with a few worthy names, mainly from the House of Lords (or rather Ladies), floated, a City man called Richard Sharp was duly appointed. After more than thirty years of expectation, that a woman might break through at last, I was rudely disappointed. Rona Fairhead was appointed to chair the BBC Trust in 2014 but her three-year term was not widely seen as a success.

Back in February 1985 I was an aspiring producer in the BBC's Current Affairs Department, as well as a first-time mum. I was photographed by the BBC's in-house magazine *Ariel,* for a feature on working mums. The photographer came to my home and took some charming pictures of me with my then eight- month old baby. He then followed me to work and took more photos of me in my office on the seventh floor of Lime Grove Studios. In one of these, I am captured at my editor's desk, in deep conversation with a female assistant producer. Quietly behind me, stands another young A.P. apparently searching for a file in a drawer. That second A.P, Mark Thompson, would become Director-General of the BBC twenty years later.

Interestingly, it was common knowledge, even then, that this young chap, on the fast-track graduate trainee scheme, was marked for great things. I cannot remember a single woman in those early years of my career ever flagged up for the same career trajectory.

Sim's glass ceiling

In the same year, 1985, one of the then most senior women in the BBC Monica Sim published a report entitled *Women in BBC Management.* (Now there's someone who after a long and distinguished BBC career, culminating as Director of Programmes, Radio, was surely a plausible candidate for the top job).

She had been commissioned to investigate the lack of progress by senior women into the top echelons by the then Director-General Alasdair Milne. At the time in the BBC's top grade there were 159 men and 6 women. Of the 263 Heads of Department, just ten per cent were women.

One of the problems Sims concluded was women's expectations of success.

She said, 'They are often not confident enough…They're too modest about their abilities because they were not brought up to push themselves forward, so they need encouraging.'

It sounds to me rather similar to what was said about women during the Gender Pay dispute in 2018 – women don't ask and so don't get. It's our fault! Well, we know how that ended with women having to put their careers on the line to take the BBC to court to prove that it was the BBC – and not the women – who were the faulty ones.

My testimony to Sim

I was one of the women working at the BBC back in the day who contributed to Ms Sim's report. I have a letter from her thanking me for my 'most helpful submission'. Not surprisingly, given my then concern about the difficulties of combining a BBC career with motherhood, I focussed on that.

This is a short extract from what I wrote at the time:

'Most organisations, and the BBC is no exception have a career structure that assumes an uninterrupted period of full-time service whereby ambitious employees rise at regular intervals up the rungs of the hierarchy….

Married women are further disadvantaged by the unwritten assumption that those who wish to get on will be prepared to put the BBC at all times unreservedly first, before family and all other outside life. The workaholic syndrome flourishes – marriages don't.'

I suggested more opportunities for part-time working, the establishment of workplace nurseries and retraining courses specifically for women returning after long periods of childcare. Hardly radical stuff when I think about it now, but not back in the mid-eighties. Oh, and yes of course, there was Margaret Thatcher – a married woman with children indeed – in 10 Downing Street at the time.

In response to the Sim report, the best part of a year later, the BBC's action plan sounds strangely familiar – and underwhelming: an annual audit of senior staff, setting up new women-only courses in management training and technical operations; official approval for job-sharing and the appointment of an equal opportunities officer to look at the development of women and ethnic minorities within the BBC. More than thirty-five years later, how would you say that's going?

And today?

Well, to be fair, there have been huge improvements in the number of women (if not of people from ethnic minorities) in positions of influence and commissioning power, especially in creative areas. Several women have run channels and been Directors of TV and Radio. A couple have been COOs, Chief Operating Officers. And yet, none, even now, have broken through to the top CEO- level job of Director-General. Can it seriously be argued that there has not been a woman with the talent, skills and experience to do the top job?

Why did the likes of Liz Forgan, Jenny Abramsky, Helen Boaden, Lorraine Heggessey, Caroline Thomson and Jay Hunt, not make it? I haven't even started on those women who have made a huge success of running independent production companies or other media groups, who would have made excellent candidates. Maybe in the end some of this list didn't want the often thankless task of being Director-General – but not all, surely?

Does it really matter I hear some of you saying? Would the course of the BBC especially in recent years, have been any different with women at the helm?

First of all, I would say to those readers thinking that, would you say this if you were to substitute 'a man of colour' instead of 'women' in the last sentence. No, you wouldn't dare. Conversely, my focus on women in this article, shouldn't be taken to mean that I don't think it is equally scandalous that so few men or women of colour have made it to the senior levels of power at the BBC and other media institutions in this country.

Macho Management-is there another way?

I shall give you two examples of where I think a woman at the top might have brought a different approach to some of the trickier issues, particularly those involving conflict with the Government of the day (and not just Conservative ones.)

Let's consider the most recent of those, the Bashir scandal.

Reading Lord Dyson's report on what happened in 1995 and the following year when suspicion fell on the methods used by this now notorious *Panorama* reporter to obtain the interview with Princess Diana, I felt an overpowering whiff of testosterone arising from its pages.

With one exception, all the senior managers at the BBC at the time who had a role in investigating the affair internally were male. Nearly all were men who I would describe as 'clubbable', ambitious, well-schooled in the arts of corporate P.R and, perhaps, prone to confusing the interests of the BBC – and even their own personal ones -with the public interest. Decent men, highly-intelligent men yes, but as we would now say liable to corporate 'group-think'.

I am willing to bet my lifetime of licence-fee payments that not a single one of them would have thought back in 1996, or even in 1997, of the possible effect of their reporter's deception on two vulnerable young boys, who happened to be Princes of the Realm. I honestly think someone with more emotional intelligence, who might have also been female, might just have thought of that.

I can recall another major moment when the BBC and the Government were locked in a testosterone-fuelled battle. That was the period around the time of the Hutton Report in 2004 which savaged the BBC for its supposed role in the death of David Kelly.Once again, it seemed that men of a certain age and tribal loyalties to their institutions, the Labour Government on the one hand and the BBC on the other, were squaring up. It did not end well for the BBC as both the Chairman, Gavyn Davies and the DG, Greg Dyke, were forced to resign.

Maybe things would have not turned out differently in either case but we have never had a chance to find out what the top- team at the BBC would feel like and achieve, if either the Chair or the DG or – heaven forfend – both were women. In my experience of other public- service bodies, the relationship between the Chair and the CEO sets the tone for the whole organisation.

While I wish the latest male double act, Tim Davie and Richard Sharp, all the best, I am disappointed that we have not had the opportunity in twenty-first century Britain, to observe a more obviously different couple leading the BBC. It certainly needs a fresh approach as its centenary year comes ever nearer with its continuing success, even its very survival, threatened as never before.

About the contributor

Fiona Chesterton had a long career in broadcasting, at both the BBC and Channel Four. She has now returned to her first passion of writing. She has made contributions to several 'hackademic' books on media themes including *What Price Channel 4?* And *The Virus and the Media.* Her first book *'Secrets Never to be Told'* will be published by Conrad Press later this summer.

Chapter 15

No More Marking their own homework: The BBC and audience complaints.

Professor Ivor Gaber reports from both sides of the BBC complaints' system – complained against and complaints investigator. It could not last and it didn't, so along came Ofcom

Picture the scene: a run-down office in a run-down building in a run-down street in a run-down part of London – you've got it, the offices of BBC TV's daily current affairs programme '*Nationwide*' in Lime Grove, Shepherds Bush; and within it, the cubby- hole that housed its investigative slot '*Watchdog*'.

The phone rings – no email in those days. It's a senior BBC panjandrum, telling me that we appear to have committed "an inadvertent libel' and the alleged victim has made a complaint (though, thankfully, not a legal action). The panjandrum is calling me in her role as Assistant to the Director General. She is required to respond, so could I send her full details?

The details were that in a piece about a dodgy removals company a BBC cameraman, commissioned to take some street scenes in Cambridge to cover a scripting point had, inadvertently, included a removal van with the company logo clearly visible. Had the producer of the item (me) seen the footage before transmission then he might have noticed, but unfortunately he was in a different part of the rabbit warren that was Lime Grove, finalising the script.

And this formed the basis of my response to the complaint, including an apology for the oversight. My note when back and forwards a few times, with the DG's Assistant suggesting a few changes to ensure that the matter was dealt with once and for all.

Matter not closed

Having heard nothing for several months I assumed that my apology had ended the matter – but that was not to be the case. Another phone call from the same panjandrum eventually came informing me that the removals company had not been satisfied by my response and had launched a formal complaint; so, she asked, could I now respond to the latest letter of complaint.

I thanked her for letting me know and suggested that rather than repeating the rather lengthy to-ing and fro-ing by internal post, perhaps we could meet face-to-face to discuss our response.

"Sorry Ivor that's not possible." she told me. "When I last spoke to you it was in my role as assistant to the Director General, I'm now speaking to you as Secretary to the Complaints Board, so I can know nothing about our previous dealings and cannot offer you any assistance"

It was a world of Alice-in-Wonderland mirrors. Here was the same person, in possession of the same information, at one moment acting as cheerleader for the BBC and in the next as the equivalent of the clerk to the court of my 'trial'.

In the event, the matter was easily resolved with the complainant accepting a formal BBC apology, as opposed to my 'producer's apology' and I forgot about the whole incident; though no doubt somewhere deep in the underground bunker that hides all those BBC files that, somehow or other, cannot be unearthed despite Freedom of Information requests (yes I did ask) is, no doubt, one with a mark against my name headed 'Removals'.

BBC equals judge, BBC equals jury

That was my last encounter with the clearly anomalous situation of the BBC being both judge and jury in complaints made against it, until many years later when I was appointed as one of the BBC Trust's 'Independent Editorial Advisers'. The Trust, formed in 2007, was supposed to have resolved all the ambiguities of BBC governance. It did no such thing. It simply created another BBC organisation a few hundred yards down the road from Broadcasting House, nor did it solve the basic problem of the BBC 'marking its own homework'.

In fairness, having witnessed and participated in the BBC Complaints system at the Trust, it would be churlish not acknowledge that the Corporation took complaints-handling impressively seriously. And this applied to whoever, or wherever the complaint was coming from. I always noted, with a mixture of admiration, but also perplexity, how the BBC expanded significant resources in dealing with a complaint, say about its coverage of the Israel/Palestine issue (not an uncommon subject of investigation), from an organised pressure group, on one side or the other, based in Washington DC.

The Trust dealt with appeals about complaints that had gone through the BBC's intimidatingly lengthy and comprehensive complaints procedure but had left the complainant still unhappy. It did not consider every appeal, indeed its main criterion for undertaking an investigation was if a complaint raised "a matter of substance".

Who brought football to England?

My favourite 'matter of substance' was when I was asked to investigate a complaint about a BBC TV News interview aired prior to the World Cup in Brazil, in which Roy Hodgson, then manager of the England football team observed that football had been brought to that country by an Englishman (Charles Miller). The complaint came from a passionate historian of Scottish football who queried the ancestry of Miller (he had both English and Scottish antecedents). My research, in the British Library no less, revealed that neither were right and that football first arrived in Brazil via French Jesuit missionaries. Not a result that would have pleased either the complainant or Mr Hodgson. And I remained puzzled as to what 'matter of substance' it raised.

Having said that, it has to be noted that the staff at the Trust, and the Trustees, who were the ultimate arbiters of complaints that had managed to work their way through the BBC complaints system, all took their roles extremely seriously. There was no doubting the integrity and efficiency that they brought to their work and, in my experience, I believe that their judgements would have robustly stood up to any independent investigation.

However, and it's a big however, as I wrote my reports I often wondered how it might feel to be one of the complainants, all of whom must have felt sufficiently strongly about their complaint to have pursued it as far as the Trust. Had I had any personal contact with a complainant, which was actively discouraged, I feel sure I would have found it difficult to reassure them that the appeals process was 'completely independent'.

Who was the judge, who was on the jury?

They would only have had to look at the composition of the Trust's Editorial Standards Committee, which adjudicated on the appeals, to have had their doubts reinforced. In its last incarnation, before it was abolished in 2017, the Committee consisted of five members, three of whom were former BBC journalists of varying levels of seniority. And although I have no comparable figures, based on my observations I would think that the majority of the independent editorial advisers were also former BBC staffers. So not only must it have felt very much like the BBC was still marking its own homework, it was. On the other hand, with the BBC as the UK's national broadcaster, it was inevitable that a significant number of people working for the Trust, and acting as editorial advisers, would (and should) have a background in broadcasting

And the new Ofcom process?

On the face of it, *Ofcom* – now responsible for regulating the BBC – could have a similar problem; 10 of the 17 members of its Content Board, which oversees complaints, have significant BBC experience. Again it makes sense, but again it must create a problem in the minds of the complainants.

Ofcom, in its new role of regulating the BBC, has its work cut out. It must be seen to be fair to both complainants and the Corporation. How it does that without appearing to favour one side or the other is the real crunch point. But the omens are hopeful. *Ofcom* has been regulating the other public service broadcasters for the best part of two decades and, with one or two minor exceptions, has done it in a way that has sustained the confidence of both the public and the broadcasters. Adding the BBC to its current load should not cause Ofcom significant problems, unless that is, the Government continues its unwelcome interventions into the broadcasting ecology causing the good ship public service broadcasting to keel over and sink without trace. Let's hope that such a gloomy prognostication does not come to pass.

About the contributor

Ivor Gaber is Professor of Political Journalism at the University of Sussex. His previous career as a broadcast journalist encompassed senior (and not so senior) stints at BBC TV and Radio, ITV, Channel Four and Sky. He was an independent editorial adviser to the BBC Trust from 2010 until its closure in 2017.

Chapter 16

The BBC is 100. Hurrah! Long live the BBC?

A sad tale of how the new world came to appropriate the electronic crown jewels of the old world. Media entrepreneur Bernard Clark reports

Let's raise our glasses to another hundred years of Suez Crises; the firing of one Director-General by the Thatcher-loyal Marmaduke Hussey; the firing of another DG, (and BBC Chairman), at the behest of a fervent, rampaging, government press supremo; followed recently by the traducing of yet another retired Director-General because of a brilliant interview with an able and willing Princess Diana – the critics using twenty-five years of myopic hindsight.

This is BBC-BAU – business as usual – at war with the Government. Long live the BBC

Such 'incidents' had one thing in common. The lapdogs of the Press, those paragons of virtue, truth and journalistic courage, were yapping away at the Government's ankles, generally setting the 'Bash-the-BBC' agenda.

But, actually, it's not such a terrible hardship for a hundred years of brilliant public service, of digging out as much of the truth as lawyers would allow, of Nation speaking global peace unto Nation – however much the home fires were burning with ersatz, tabloid indignation.

Hurrah! Again, long live the......

Except, there won't be another hundred years, maybe not even twenty.

Because, while our beloved BBC was ducking and diving, it was fighting the previous war, or even the one before that, against the wrong enemy.

The real war was about *scale*, not journalistic objectivity, but because the BBC is largely a civil service organisation, inured in the soft under-belly of Whitehall, it carried on battling Grub Street and the Government, while an unseen enemy from across the Atlantic, who hadn't even been invented at the beginning of the twenty-first century, gradually amassed Aunties' crown jewels, to become practically unassailable.

2009: Year zero

It's possible, accurately, to date the year this war was lost by the BBC. 2009. Remember where you were then?

In 2005/6, the BBC had 'lucked into', or otherwise invented, designed and developed, the broadcasting equivalent of the A-Bomb, also known as the *iPlayer*. Overseen by a designer called Ben Lavender, this was a British innovation with such enormous implications you'd have thought that everyone in the chain of command, from the Prime Minster down, would sink to their knees with gratitude and excitement.

The opposite happened.

The BBC went into full bureaucratic mode, terrified by the constant, draining tut-tuts from their play-safe copyright lawyers, embarking on meeting after meeting after meeting about the likely accusations of state-funded, monopolistic, 'market bullying'.

At this time, it was only the BBC's fear of fear itself – the Murdochian/Harmsworth machines hadn't yet cottoned on to the power and potential of streaming that the *iPlayer* could bring into everyone's living rooms, let alone smart phones.

From a nervous BBC perspective, it was as if a brilliant technician had 'plopped a turd into the teapot', to quote one particularly colourful BBC Chairman.

Meanwhile, across the Atlantic, *Netflix* was still a DVD distribution company, only using the internet so that customers could order what was on offer; the actual films would be sent on DVD, through the post. But it's likely they were well aware of the potential revolution the BBC had developed in London.

There follows three years of missed opportunities and tragedy. Apart from the hugely talented and dynamic IT engineers, there are no heroes here, only hapless Jobsworths – in the BBC, the Department of Culture, the Treasury and, ultimately, in the UK Competition Commission.

A kangaroo comes along

Enter the ridiculously named *Project Kangaroo*.

As with all things ground-breaking and revolutionary, the BBC senior management was timid and snail-like. Afraid of proclaiming a wonderful, world-beating, new BBC streaming service, they went for safety in numbers. The BBC joined up with ITV and Channel 4, to nullify the likely opposition, and for good measure presented *Kangaroo* as educational and archive based – a 'good-for-you' project that Whitehall was bound to back.

But now the Murdochian interests saw the danger to their own semi-monopolies, and the big guns of the educational publishing world weighed in, until the lobbyists had completely changed the agenda in Westminster.

No longer was this a world-beating British invention that would benefit the people, and allow the UK to take the lead in what would soon be a major new global media industry. Through lobbying smoke and whispers, it had become an unfair, non-competitive monopoly.

In 2008, the Office of Fair Trading reported *Project Kangaroo* to the Competition Commission.

Meanwhile, again, on the other side of the Atlantic, the real competition to this world-beating project was striding forward. With its DVD-by-mail service suffering intense competition from *Amazon* and *Apple*, *Netflix* originated its own, albeit very limited, streaming service in 2007, significantly behind the *iPlayer*. But they were catching up.

Then in 2009, *Project Kangaroo* was unceremoniously canned – at exactly the moment and *Netflix* launched a much wider service in the US.

Why was the kangaroo killed?

It's worth looking in detail at the Competition Commission's decision on *Kangaroo,* announced by Chairman Peter Freeman, CBE, QC, a British establishment figure of impeccable lineage.

'This joint venture would be too much of a threat to competition in this developing market and has to be stopped'.

Freeman's idea of competition seemed to stop at Dover. In one of the most inwardly xenophobic and ridiculous decisions of all time, there is virtually no mention of the real competition from five thousand miles away.

In the global media battle of Britain against the World – the World, (i.e. *Netflix, Amazon* and the US corporate broadcasters) just got awarded half a dozen penalties, when Britain were four goals up. Hurrah for the special relationship.

About a hundred, highly motivated *Kangaroo* staff were dispatched to the waste bin, and the streaming centre of gravity moved from London to California – never to return.

The BBC aren't blameless in this tragedy of errors. It was their endless, fruitless, indecisive, meetings culture, along with their cloying cosiness with Whitehall, which led to them stabbing themselves in their own back. Had they just 'got on with it', followed the talent and the innovators, the BBC's streaming service would be world beating by now.

Next time you watch the circular nothingness of *W1A*, think of *Project Kangaroo*, and be prepared to weep.

Netflix did not stand still

To add insult to injury, Reed Hastings, the Netflix owner and guru, had developed a management/HR philosophy* that would illustrate *Netflix* strengths and the BBC's grave weaknesses – a document which is a frightening blueprint for why the BBC failed so badly while holding a winning hand.

It has little to do with broadcasting or specifically the media, but has at its core a route-map for creative management in a time of technological innovation and change, all within a fiercely dynamic landscape. If you care about Britain, and compare it to what you know of management at the BBC, keep the Kleenex handy.

Some extracts:

'At Netflix we particularly value the following nine behaviours and skills in

our colleagues:

- *Judgment*
- *Communication*
- *Impact – (one sub-part here is especially poignant. 'You exhibit bias-to-action, and avoid analysis-paralysis').*
- *Curiosity*
- *Innovation*
- *Courage*
- *Passion*
- *Honesty*
- *Selflessness'.*

Netflix Culture Deck, 2009 – still available online, feel free to look it up. https://www.slideshare.net/reed2001/culture-1798664

Seemingly, nothing earth-shattering here, nothing that might hint at the eclipse of a global broadcasting powerhouse by a fledgling competitor.

The BBC culture deck?

But now flip the desired *Netflix* behaviours around, through 180-degrees, and you can see that the BBC rewards the polar opposite in most of the skills. Believe me, I know – having spent twenty years working there. It is why I, and many of my passionate, innovative, impactful, decisive, courageous colleagues left, just when we were at our most valuable.

Here's the BBC culture deck

- Judgment – try never to make a decision

- Communication – secrecy is everything

- Impact – keep your head down – use analysis-paralysis

- Curiosity – leave that to the programme Wallahs

- Innovation – danger! The road to me being made redundant

- Courage – if you've got it, leave for independent production

- Passion – once-upon-a-time-ago

- Honesty – that's for BBC programmes, not management

- Selflessness – I think that means what's best for me?

Anyone who has spent much time there, knows that BBC Culture penalises all of the *Netflix* virtues, in favour of avoiding decisions and accountability. Most entitled managers see it as part of its child-like charm – but in a non-entitled world, it has sowed the seeds of BBC destruction.

Cold figures are even worse

Given this book is meant to be about celebrating a hundred years of the BBC, the questions then move to – can the BBC survive, should it survive? The bean-counters' figures are not reassuring.

The present market capitalisation of *Netflix* is $222billion. In 2002 it was $222million, so in the last twenty years, *Netflix* has grown a thousand-fold – *a 100,000 per cent increase.*

In the same time, the BBC turnover has gone from £3billion in 2002, to £5.5billion in 2020 – *an increase of 67 per cent.*

Spending on programmes

Clearly, market capitalisation isn't the whole story, but if you look at spending on content, the figures are no better.

Netflix didn't begin spending on original programming until 2009, in which year its spent US$110million. This year it will spend US$11.8 billion – an increase of 10,000 per cent in ten years. The equivalent for the BBC is 2009 £4.8billion to 2020 £4.9billion. i.e., 2 per cent.

Perhaps even more pertinent, *Netflix* originates programmes in thirty different languages, and makes them available in sixty different languages – all perfectly possible for the BBC through the international i*Player*, but that's before the global bus left town.

In case this is seen as malicious criticism of the BBC in its centenary year, it is nothing of the sort. I began my working life at the BBC, like a large number of *Netflix*'s talented programme makers, and many of us still work for both organisations and love them in equal measure.

But on issues of governance – that gentlemanly nonsense by which the British establishment controls too much of our lives – I think of the BBC as full of villains, yes villains. From the members of the Executive Committee down to middle management, they are weak, indecisive, compliant figures who have been shoe-horned into supervisory roles, and stand up neither to Government, nor the life-timers inside the BBC.

As you might expect, the Netflix culture deck has a way of dealing with such 'well-meaning' folk.

'Inadequate performance gets a generous severance package.'

The BBC has a lot to learn, and learn quickly, if it wants another hundred years of life.

About the contributor

Bernard Clark joined the BBC in 1968, then left in the early eighties to join the 'Independent Revolution' with the advent of Channel 4. His company, L10N Media now works across over twenty countries, servicing the BBC, Netflix, and most of the US majors.

Chapter 17

Netflix is not the BBC

Social commentator Peter York explains why comparisons between Netflix (and the other 'California streamers') and the BBC are wrong and, at best, confused

People who talk about Netflix as a 'digital' substitute for the 'analogue' BBC are, in my view, either deeply confused, completely lame-brained or simply dishonest. In reality, Netflix and the other US 'streamers' are about as unlike the BBC as it's possible to be. Let me explain.

California is not Britain...

The first difference is that the British Broadcasting Corporation is by, with, from and for *Britain. Netflix* (with a foot in Silicon Valley and a foot in Hollywood) just isn't – it's as Californian as *Google,* Meghan Markle, Donald Duck and the Golden Gate Bridge.

Secondly (and it's embarrassing to have to point this out) *the BBC is a public service broadcaster* – in fact, it wrote the playbook for public service broadcasting. It's universally available to British audiences on every TV, radio and online platform, giving *everyone* a vast range of local and national content and shared experiences that inform and educate as well as entertain – universality is the principle; the point of the BBC. *Netflix* will never do that – and, as a private, listed US company, why should it?

Netflix is *only* distributed online,[12] so only those with broadband even have the option of subscribing to it. For those who do so, its huge, debt-funded content budget allows it to buy and create some wonderful programmes – as well as a lot of standard stuff. But they're all from the new technology version of a deep freeze: global, with a long shelf life and entertaining – like Disney, now its biggest competitor. If you're old enough to remember video rentals, it's like a much better, 21st Century, high-tech version of Blockbuster.

---

[12] Using Subscriber Video On Demand (SVOD)

There's next to no live or local TV or radio and no public service content (again, why would they?).

It's a great addition to British media choices – but it isn't the BBC.

What about Netflix's UK productions?

But hold on, you say, Netflix now 'originates' (it uses the term rather flexibly)[13] programmes, including in Britain, using our brilliant actors, technicians and studios. Sometimes – most famously in *The Crown* – they're about Britain. But well under half of its output is 'original' (even under its flexible definition) and most of that is not made here. So although *The Crown* is a big part of what it *publicises*, it's only a small part of what it actually *does*, which is mostly stuff from the freezer. It's like all those Hollywood movie productions which use our world-class resources but where the credit and worldwide profits go to America.

Netflix operates in 190 countries and its business model is mostly about creating global scale via content with – as far as possible – global audience appeal. *The Crown* is about the best-known Brits (and family) in the world. Those of us able to watch it, because we have broadband, a smart TV and a *Netflix* subscription, enjoy much of what it offers. *Call My Agent* is brilliant. But it's not there to give you *live* – say, national news – or fresh – new British drama or documentary – never mind *local*. Nothing like BBC Wales or BBC Radio Stoke-on-Trent.

None of this is a criticism. *Netflix* and the other US streamers increase competition and choice. But they're very different from the British broadcasters[14], and they have significant downsides – driving up the cost of content and eroding our national culture.[15]

---

13 For instance, it describes Bodyguard (commissioned by the BBC and produced by ITV) as a 'Netflix Original' in the territories for which it bought the rights.
14 BBC, ITV, C4, C5 and Sky.
15 A recent Enders Analysis report showed that, while the growth of co-productions (to protect UK broadcasters' programme budgets) may already be reducing the number of British expressions, idioms and reference points – 'Geordie accent', 'land girls', 'dosh', 'Wagamama' – in their drama and comedy programmes, it's still far higher than on the UK-produced shows commissioned by the US streamers. Tom Harrington and Tom Standen-Jewell, 'Outsourcing culture: When British shows aren't British', Enders Analysis, 7 February 2021.

What's the real game?

The real game that's being played when people praise *Netflix* – as they did HBO in its time – and denigrate the BBC is a mixture of half-baked technological determinism and standard-issue Beeb-bashing by right-wing politicians, newspapers and those think-tanks that tend towards non-transparent funding. Much of it derives from an unholy combination of ideology – that 'all Public Service Anything is bad', an invention of 'cultural Marxism' or some such – and (invariably undeclared) commercial vested interests: their newspaper's proprietor or possibly the think tank's very discreet donors would love to make profits from the BBC's big audiences (despite their constantly saying no one watches it anymore because they've all switched to *Netflix* and *YouTube*).

But attacking the BBC and championing overseas commercial vested interests isn't a good look, as we know from discussions of the NHS. So the funding sources are played down and the faux-academic reports and reasonable-sounding 'why-oh-why' pieces say the Beeb 'was wonderful in its time' but has now outlived its usefulness because there's lots of lovely stuff like *Netflix* around. This argument doesn't survive much examination – but who's doing the examining?

What the BBC does and Netflix doesn't

Just think what the BBC actually does and Netflix doesn't. *Netflix* won't be there to help teach your children *'Bite Sized'* in lockdown at a moment's notice. It won't be there for the Government's Covid-19 press conferences. It won't be there with investigative consumer programmes to find the people who cheated your mum out of her savings. And it won't be there to film the choir your wife has started singing with in a small town. It has no Royal Charter mandated 'public purposes', constantly examined by Ofcom and Select Committees like the BBC. It is a totally profit-maximising entity, largely unregulated, very well managed, but not a substitute for the BBC.

The BBC, despite the Government having cut its public funding[16] by 30 per cent in real (inflation-adjusted) terms since 2010, is still the largest single investor in British TV content from all those British talents and the heart of our very successful broadcasting ecology. For every pound we give it, it generates at least £2.69 in increased economic activity, according

---

[16] Mainly licence fee income after 'top-slicing' for other purposes.

to PriceWaterhouseCoopers[17] – almost up there with the Ronettes' 'For every kiss you give me I'll give you three'.[18]

And it's central to the UK's 'soft power', with *BBC News,* the *BBC World Service* – and all the British programmes and formats it sells abroad, bringing in big money for UK independent producers and much-needed extra cash for its own budgets. The BBC puts Britain on the world stage.

And, even with its greatly reduced resources, it still makes fantastic drama: *I May Destroy You, Line of Duty, Killing Eve, Call the Midwife, Fleabag* all in the recent past. Plus five orchestras, 39 local radio stations, the UK's most trusted news website, *The Repair Shop* and *Gardener's Question Time.*

The BBC pulls it off for challenging drama and rooted British traditional obsessions. *Netflix* is great as an add-on to the BBC and other British broadcasters. It is not, and never will be, a substitute for them:

	BBC	Netflix
Nationality	British	American
Ownership	The British public (licence fee payers), Public body	Shareholders – American quoted company
Platform(s)	Everything: Broadcast TV, Broadcast Radio, Online SVOD (News site etc), Live events (concerts etc)	Streaming (SVOD)
UK regulator	Ofcom	None (yet)
Public purposes	Five major 'public purposes' set out in Royal Charter	No mandatory public purposes
Primary Market	British public	Global – 190 nations

17 Patrick Barwise and Peter York, The War Against the BBC, Penguin, November 2020, p35.
18 The Ronettes, Be My Baby (1963).

Audience		
Secondary Audiences	British programmes for overseas (News, World Service)	Global – 190 nations
Headquarters (world)	London	Los Gatos, California
Headquarters (Europe)	London	Amsterdam

And another thing – Netflix is *much* 'wokier' than the 'woke BBC'

Many of those saying that, now we have Netflix, we no longer need the BBC, '… a 20th century construct trying to survive in the fast-paced digital world of the 21st century',[19] also constantly attack it for being too 'woke' – the big new red-button hate word among right-wing culture warriors like *GB News*.

Leaving aside the question of how many of these sages could actually explain the difference between analogue and digital media, the paradox about them attacking the BBC for its 'wokeness' while seeing *Netflix* as the market solution of their dreams is that – on top of all the other differences – *Netflix* is *much, much* 'wokier' than the BBC.

This was spelt out by Damian Reilly in the *Spectator* in March 2020: 'If you think the BBC is too woke for you, just wait until you sample wokeness as beamed into your sitting room by *Netflix* – maker of programmes like *Dear White People* ("students of colour navigate the daily slights and slippery politics of life at an Ivy League college that's not nearly as 'post racial' as it thinks")'.

He added, 'imagine the outcry if the BBC refused to make programmes in places whose abortion laws they didn't agree with, as *Netflix* recently threatened to do in the state of Georgia'.[20]

---

[19] Rob Wilson, 'Time to face up and front up for the BBC', Chapter 9 (pages 55-9) in *Is the BBC STILL in Peril? Advice to the New Director-General* (Bite-Sized Books, 2020), edited by John Mair and Tom Bradshaw. The quotation is from the first sentence of the chapter.
[20] Damian Reilly, 'Forget the BBC – it's Netflix and Amazon that are "woke"', *Spectator*, 18 March 2020.

Netflix's 'wokeness' is now even clearer. Of course we don't *know* what the BBC's critics would have said if it, not Netflix, had broadcast *Bridgerton*. Perhaps they would have praised the realistic, full-on sex scenes and the casting of black actors in so many royal and aristocratic roles in a Regency costume drama.[21]

And if the BBC, not Netflix, had shown *The Crown*, with its vicious portrayal of the royals as hidebound, snobbish dimwits talking in a strangulated parody of posh British English, perhaps these critics would still have focused on the high-quality acting and production. Perhaps.

What is less debateable is that Netflix is full of Californian 'wokery', including about the need to share your feelings and speak up for 'your truth'.

In the aftermath of *Oprah with Meghan and Harry*, many Americans love that (notwithstanding George Floyd's murder, the Proud Boys and all that) they are now being portrayed as less racist than the Brits, while also being shocked by the apparent ghastliness of our royals. The Oprah interview may have triggered this, but four seasons of *The Crown* surely paved the way.

So, who's wokier, the BBC or Netflix? It isn't even close: whatever you think of *Bodyguard*'s portrayal of modern Britain, *Bridgerton*'s casting of a black actor as a Regency English duke or *The Crown* showing the royals deliberately humiliating their Balmoral guests, *Netflix* wins the wokery prize by a mile.

So when someone confused tells you we don't need the BBC now we've got the lovely new 'California Streamers', or that the BBC is full of woke moaners or crazed communists just ask them a few simple questions. If the world has another pandemic, a catastrophic recession or seems to be limbering up for WW3, who you gonna call, the BBC – or a Disney cartoon princess?

About the contributor

Peter York is a management consultant, journalist and author. His latest book, co-authored with Patrick Barwise, is *The War Against the BBC: How*

---

[21] And perhaps they'd be equally enthusiastic if the BBC, not Channel Five, had cast black actors – including the lead – in its miniseries *'reimagining'* Anne Boleyn's life *'through a feminist lens… and her pushback against [a] patriarchal society'* (press release 13.4.21).

an Unprecedented Combination of Hostile Forces Is Destroying Britain's Greatest Cultural Institution... And Why You Should Care (Penguin, November 2020).

Chapter 18

The arts of the possible

Steve Clarke, the editor of *Television,* asks whether the BBC has lost the plot on arts programming

You probably noticed that Bob Dylan turned 80 on May 24, 2021. Radio 4 celebrated the anniversary with a series of five chronological essays, a drama starring Richard Curtis, Dinner with Dylan, and a documentary. Over on BBC TV this significant birthday was effectively ignored. Not a single new programme.

For diehard fans, a 1987 *Omnibus* featuring a typically eccentric, though curiously revealing interview with the greatest songwriter of the rock era was available on the *iPlayer*, but those in search of fresh BBC insights into the man who redefined the popular song had no choice but to go to Radio 4.

Was this an omission a blip or further evidence that for arts coverage in its widest sense *Radio 4* is nowadays regularly eclipsing BBC TV? Or to put it another way, are the arts under the new regime of DG Tim Davie safe in his modernising hands? The former leader of BBC Worldwide/BBC Studios has said a lot regarding his determination to make the BBC licence fee something that genuinely gives everyone value for their money, whether they live in Marylebone or Middlesbrough. This is a laudable aim, but we don't need Richard Hoggart to remind us that the very best of the arts has the power to appeal across all demographic and all social groups.

As *Ofcom* is only too well aware, arts are among what it refers to as an "at risk category" of programmes on the BBC. The sorry truth is that despite Tony Hall's pledge in 2014 to launch "the biggest push we've made in the arts for a generation" the regulator's analysis of the figures suggest a different story. The number of hours devoted to first-run arts programmes on BBC TV declined by 47 per cent between 2010-19. "Most notably, there were 50 fewer hours of new arts content in 2019 than in 2018," *Ofcom* added.

Not serving the super-users?

Reflecting Boris Johnson's Downing Street, has Davie perhaps declared war on those like me and my peers who tend to over-use BBC services? As *Ofcom* noted in its last 2020 Annual Report on the BBC, "older people (aged 55+) and those in higher socio-economic groups have traditionally consumed more BBC content and been more satisfied than the UK average. However, reach is decreasing among these loyal groups, and older audiences in particular are starting to show signs of decreasing satisfaction." This is a reminder of the tightrope that Davie must navigate as he seeks to re-position the BBC in an age of division and populism.

People have been griping about how BBC treats the arts for decades. The national broadcaster is our greatest cultural institution so in this respect the Beeb is fair game. The late, great, polymath, Jonathan Miller, was a vociferous critic. In 2002 he complained: "Unless you have a programme about how to decorate your house or chop up vegetables, it is impossible to get anyone in the BBC to commission your programme."

Did they lose the plot in the swinging sixties?

Several decades before the new century BBC paternalism was thankfully jettisoned. Exactly when is a moot point but it's widely accepted that the BBC's top-down approach to arts and culture was eventually torpedoed by the impact of the freewheeling 1960s.

It was that decade that gave rise to what Jean Seaton described as a "new kind of 'television intellectual'" in the shape of people like Joan Bakewell (now presenting Sky's *Portrait Artist of the Year)* and Melvyn Bragg, who served his apprenticeship on Huw Wheldon's *Monitor* before switching channels to create what would become UK TV's longest-running arts series, *The South Bank Show*, an ITV flagship for an astonishing 32 years. The programme is still aired, by *Sky Arts,* where it was revived in 2012. It is one of the ironies that a BBC-trained film maker ended up popularising the arts on ITV. Bragg's celebrated interview with dramatist Dennis Potter in 1994, visibly close to death's door, in which he revealed that he'd named his cancer "Murdoch" remains one of the most compelling interviews ever shown on British TV.

Still complaining after all these years...

Recently, those complaining most vociferously about BBC arts have tended to come from the more traditional end of the arts fraternity. In May 2021, a group of TV arts luminaires including Humphrey Burton and Tony

Palmer (both trailblazers for BBC Arts) wrote in a letter to the *Guardian* that today's BBC classical music documentaries lacked "adventure, curiosity and revelation." Could that criticism be applied to documentaries about poets and pop stars too?

Go back to September 2018 and no less a figure than David Attenborough told the *Radio Times*: "I don't think the BBC does enough [arts and culture]. It's not enough simply to say: 'Well, it doesn't get a big enough audience.' If you're a public service broadcaster, what you should be saying is: 'We will show the broad spectrum of human interest.'"

As controller of BBC 2 in the second half of the 1960s the great man had commissioned Sir Kenneth Clark's epic *Civilisation* documentary series, delivered in some thirteen 50-minute episodes. *Civilisation*, commissioned in 1966, was the first 'landmark' documentary and was unashamedly patrician. Despite this, the series was a big hit across demographic groups. Art galleries and museums reported a surge in visitors following the broadcast of each episode.

When as the incoming Director-General, Tony Hall, fresh from running the Royal Opera House, attempted to tap into the kudos of this TV watershed by pushing the BBC to make a follow-up series, *Civilisations*, broadcast in 2018, the results, a nine-parter presented variously by Simon Schama, Mary Beard and David Olusoga received decidedly mixed reviews.

BBC 3 and 4 – new homes for the arts?

Fears regarding Davie's commitment to the arts have grown since it was announced that youth-friendly *BBC3* is to return as a linear channel in 2022 and *BBC4*, once renowned for its commitment to the arts, was being downgraded to "an archive and performance channel."

Now no one expects the BBC to return to the pre-multi-channel era when arts series were regularly shown in primetime on both BBC One and BBC Two. Strange as it may now seem, *Omnibus* was once a regular fixture of *BBC One*, running from 1967-2001 before being downgraded to BBC Two, where it survived for just two years. To quote Jean Seaton again, *Omnibus* "put radical approaches to programme-making about the arts on BBC One, cherishing idiosyncratic and adventurous films."

Arena, under the guidance of Alan Yentob, went one step further as the Beatles, the Beats, the Ford Cortina and James Bond films were all regarded as cultural artefacts worthy of serious and engaging BBC film making.

These subjects appeared alongside more traditional arts subjects -writers, poets and painters like T S Eliot, W B Years and Francis Bacon. Thankfully, *Arena* isn't quite dead and continues to appear as an occasional treat, as does BBC One's *Imagine,* presented by the ubiquitous Yentob.

Some have maintained the BBC TV's arts coverage has lacked focus since the demise of *The Late Show* which morphed into *Newsnight Review/Late Review* in 2014.

Under the BBC annual plan published in March 2021, it was announced that BBC Two will become the home of the BBC's specialist programming with a renewed focus on science, history and the arts. "*BBC Two* will be enriched by taking the best of *BBC Four's* originations, giving these programmes a bigger shop window," said the plan.

"Arts will continue to be a centrepiece of *[BBC] Four* as we carry on showcasing *Culture in Quarantine* through this period. Outside the UK, we are exploring potential commercial opportunities for *BBC Four* to become a new global subscription service that takes our strengths in specialist factual [programming] to the world stage," the plan added.

As *BBC4's* (already small) budget comes under further pressure, it is hard to imagine the fall in the quantity of new arts shows being reversed. Of course, the *iPlayer* provides rich pickings to curate the enormous BBC arts archive. During the pandemic we have had *Culture In Quarantine.* It is arguable that as reality-TV inspired formats have invaded the arts, overall TV arts coverage today is more accessible than ever.

Sky does it better? Netflix Too?

Sky Arts, free to air since autumn 2020, has excelled with series like Portrait Artist of the Year. There is no shortage of music documentaries, both acquired from third parties and part financed by *Sky*; for subscribers there is a rich back catalogue of performance-based programmes across pop, rock, classical and dance. Let's not forget, *Sky* beat *Radio 4* to a Bob Dylan play by a clear four years thanks to its hilarious *Urban Myths* in which the bard of Minnesota unwittingly becomes a guest waiting for Dave the plumber, rather than musician Dave Stewart in suburban London's Crouch End.

Popular arts documentaries are there for the seeking on Netflix too, but a streamer like Netflix or Amazon is not going to find, let alone nurture the next Andrew Graham-Dixon or Waldemar Januszczak, both regular faces on BBC TV until recently. And what does it say about the BBC TV's arts coverage that the most interesting arts innovation in lockdown broadcasting came from *Channel 4* in the shape of *Grayson's Art Club*.

Future hopes and dreams for BBC arts

The worry also is that quirky, unexpected arts films, as well as more traditional series devoted to say, a style of painting or writing, are further marginalised due to lack of funds and motivation. Radio arts programmes cost a fraction of what a TV documentary does. The cynical view is that the BBC only every really ups its cultural game when Charter Renewal beckons. The present Charter is guaranteed until December 31, 2027. That doesn't mean that Tim Davie should risk diluting the loyalty of those licence fee payers who want and expect a rich and varied diet across the arts on radio, TV and online.

About the contributor

Steve Clarke edits the RTS monthly magazine, *Television* and is a regular contributor to *Variety*. He is a former editor of *Broadcast* and has written on the media and TV for all the Fleet Street broadsheets. He is co-author, with Chris Horrie, of *Fuzzy Monsters: Fear and Loathing at The BBC* (1994).

Chapter 19

Is the party over?

David Lancaster undertakes a meditation on the future of the BBC in a world of radical technological and political upheaval. He suggests that although the corporation needs to change, the big questions are how will it do it, and, above all, <u>who</u> will make the decisions?

The BBC at 100 – the questions come thick and fast. What is it? Do we still care? Are we talking about an institution that for a glorious century has embodied the ideals of public service broadcasting, or has it been a typical British bodge, whose time is well and truly up?

For those, like me, who were weaned on its' productions, and later found themselves on its' payroll, any response will be influenced by personal experience, or, worse, nostalgia. It is impossible to come to firm and objective conclusions. The best one can do is try to ask some of the right questions.

What is the BBC?

If I were to isolate one image that encapsulated my time at the Corporation, it would be the office Christmas party. Back in the Eighties, I attended these rather louche bashes in a number of grotty conference rooms round the country, and my strongest memory (apart from the vast quantities of booze we managed to knock back) was being the member of a club, maybe a slightly smug, backstabbing and arrogant club, but, still, one whose membership was hard to attain and therefore well worth having.

In other words, you had a nice, safe job. In those days, casualisation wasn't the norm; production workers were either on long-term staff contracts, or quite advantageous short-term ones. This stability in employment was reflected in the stability of the broadcasting industrial structure, a duopoly, the sort of arrangement that then PM Thatcher loathed. In one corner was the BBC, a service with a monopoly of funds gleaned from a legally enforceable licence fee, while in the other, was ITV, "the other side," to coin a term we used during my teenage years. This was funded by another monopoly, this time of TV advertising revenue. Both these giants were in pursuit of something that was often termed "the audience", or, when you were working on specific programmes, "*our* audience". This was a slippery and inconstant creature, likely to switch allegiance at any moment, but something palpably *there*, like a sausage roll on a paper plate.

But. maybe that's pushing the party metaphor too far.

Those individuals knocking back the cheap white wine might differ quite drastically in personal and professional terms, but they were united by a collection of unspoken presumptions that could be corralled into the phrase "*public service broadcasting*".

What is/was PSB?

In the case of the BBC I knew, the term meant, in essence, anything the Corporation cared to do, whether it was blatantly populist, or relatively esoteric. This confusion was inherent in the very way the institution was constructed (or cobbled together). The overriding principle was to justify what the neo-liberals would later call the "poll tax" of the licence fee. This demand, it seemed to me then and still does now, could be met in two contradictory ways – first, by creating programmes that attracted large audiences in a market- driven "bums on seats" formula, or by bucking that very same market, showing some vaguely defined "quality" and "innovation" in its programming, and thus provide what the market *could* not.

The trouble is the Corporation has never resolved this tension. To fall once again into anecdotage – I can remember, as a trainee, going to a seminar for news and current affairs hacks. This was the early Eighties, when the BBC was bursting a blood vessel to launch *Breakfast Time* ahead of its commercial rival *TV-AM*. The argument was that if the audience did not watch its news on BBC1 first thing in the morning, it wouldn't watch anything else the channel offered.

A few years later, I attended another talk. Here, the group was made up of representatives from Light Entertainment (the producers responsible for comedy and sketch shows), along with people from the Natural History Unit (the name of Sir David Attenborough was synonymous with the genre even then) and the people in Presentation (the unsung department responsible for trailers and announcements). We were addressed by a very high up executive, who made it abundantly clear that if the BBC didn't defend to the death its right to make situation comedies and popular dramas, then it would be closing time in the gardens and watering holes of West London, or the rest of the country for that matter.

The odd thing is that both these positions were equally valid. In this sense, the BBC has always been a broken-backed creature.

Things change

Now we have casualisation, fragmentation, and, above all, the profit motive: the shades of Margaret Thatcher and her friends must be clapping their ghostly hands in glee. For they have slain their dragons; cosy stitch ups have been replaced by multiple providers with different voices; producer interests have given way to audience needs; above all, there is the free-market fetish of "choice" – Video on Demand on any device you care to name; more programmes then you can shake your remote control at, whether they be dramatic, "reality", or conventional documentary.

Add to this the vloggers, the Twitter gang, the Tik-Tokkers, the Instagram posse, the citizen journalists, nice and cheap on YouTube – you, the viewer, pays your money and you takes your choice.

Spoilt for choice?

In terms of drama, the algorithms encourage you to watch the same sort of programme. Meanwhile, for the viewer in search of reliable reporting and current affairs analysis, the vloggers sometimes elide independent commentary and advertising; citizen journalists muddy the waters of impartiality and bias; *Netflix, Apple, Amazon Prime, Disney +* – all are large media corporations, itching to become as close to monopoly as the market will let them. It's a mad world, my masters. The audience can no longer be perceived as one creature. So, the next question is…

What does the BBC do in the future?

Actually, that question should be framed more pessimistically; it should say, "What's going to get *done* to the BBC?" The answer depends on your priorities. On the one hand, the streaming services are doing a very good job at well-funded drama and entertainment, although we may come to regret the dominance of a limited number of international conglomerates. That remains to be seen. For factual viewers, on the other hand, market fragmentation means, not opportunity, but confusion – and the confusion is occurring right now. When it comes to news, current affairs and documentary, whom do we trust?

One of the most interesting things about teaching media and communication is that though students have been brought up in this increasingly fragmented and commercial environment, they still retain a race memory, if you like, of core journalistic values, which come straight out of the BBC Editorial Guidelines. These include impartiality, accuracy and fair dealing. It is good that these principles are still alive, though whether they are shared by general viewers, or practised by students once they join the workforce, is very hard to say.

So, in a world of barnstormers and demagogues, should we still cling to what some might see as these patrician and condescending ideals – in short, keep the BBC's core news values and leave everything else to the market?

I can hear the howls of pain from artists and comedians and performers, who want the latitude to experiment and fail. Moreover, should we ditch the compulsory licence fee, let the BBC decide on its own output, and turn it into a subscription service where, in effect, the audience votes with its wallet? Or do we have a pot of public money for which programme makers can bid with ideas for a "public service" programme? That leads to another question:

Who decides that?

Politicians?

God forbid.

The other BBC

Then again, what about radio? The World Service? It is one thing to say that the BBC needs to restrain its expansionist tendencies and concentrate on areas that commercial operations can't provide, and quite another to work out what this means in practice.

The solutions are elusive, but two things can be gloomily predicted. First, viewers wanting a range of work – someone, say, who likes *Strictly Come Dancing*, but would appreciate a decent production of *The Cherry Orchard* – is likely to find themselves considerably frustrated, or out of pocket. Secondly, those office Christmas parties of the future will be attended by an ever-shifting cast of freelance characters, less experienced, more afraid for their jobs and therefore less adventurous in their programme making.

And so?

In a sense, this whole piece has been avoiding the fundamental issue of who gets to work in the industry. Forty years ago, when I applied to the organisation, it was made very clear that the BBC did not encourage something called "elitism". Yet what was the institution in those days, but a group of white men deciding on what was good for the public? None of that insularity has fundamentally changed. Irrespective of institutional issues, the people with power are failing to broaden the party's guest list. What do we do about this? That is the final, ultimate, and most unsettling question.

About the contributor.

David Lancaster is a Senior Teaching Fellow in the School of Media and Communication at the University of Leeds. Before that, he worked as a producer both for the BBC and for independent companies. At various times, he has produced general magazine programmes, breakfast television, news and current affairs discussions, a quiz and a comedy series.

Chapter 20

Levelling up: Making the BBC personally relevant again

Dr Liam McCarthy argues that for the BBC to survive into its second century it needs to become relevant again across the UK by physically and emotionally moving out of London, spreading its journalistic firepower across the country and embracing growing digital literacy among consumers to deliver significant digital local news services.

Others have written about the potential of the BBC to play an important part in portraying 'global Britain' as an important component of British 'soft power'. However, to do this it has first to survive charter renewal in 2027 and that means it must become more relevant and valued right across the United Kingdom.

A London centric BBC, equally denigrated by a competitive British media and disenfranchised licence fee payers, will be in no fit state to portray Britain to the world. This essay argues for a greater 'levelling up' of the BBC making it closer to communities across the country – a local and less metropolitan BBC as the flip side to a global BBC.

The BBC should really move out of London

According to the BBC at the beginning of 2020 half of its staff were based in Greater London – a region that accounts for just 13 per cent of the UK population. In England alone eight in ten people live outside London, yet the city dominates the BBC mindset. To be fair to Director-General Tim Davie his latest plans in 2021 to distribute more staff across the country go further and include editorial highlights such as presenting at least one third of editions of the *Today* programme from outside the capital – something I called for in *The BBC A Winter of Discontent?*[22] But the BBC needs to go further. News happens where journalists, cameras and microphones are which is why we seem to get more news on the BBC from the USA than the north of England. All BBC journalism posts should be spread across

---

[22] L. McCarthy, 'Bottom Up. Re-building the BBC.' In J. Mair (Ed.), *The BBC a Winter of Discontent?* (Bite-Sized Books: Goring, 2020).

the country to reflect the population and regional specialisms; there isn't a BBC London Correspondent so why should there be a Northern Correspondent? This is not a dig at the brilliant Judith Moritz, the current BBC Northern Correspondent, but just think of the stories that reporters based in all British cities could bring to the national news. Understanding the nation as a whole rather than just from a London centric view is why it is important that the BBC spreads out across the UK. These moves should not be limited and should include senior roles within the corporation – it is patronising to suggest that the best people can only be found in London.

Renew BBC local and regional journalism

There is a market failure in local print and commercial radio journalism and a growing democratic deficit in which politicians and local leaders are not being held to account. Media consolidation in the UK has resulted in four out of five newspapers and four out of five commercial local radio companies being owned by just seven companies. Journalism is expensive and this consolidation of ownership has led to owners hollowing out local newsrooms to save money. In the last 15 years more than 250 local newspapers have closed and over 200 local radio stations have been subsumed into national brands such as *Greatest Hits Radio, Smooth* and *Capital*.[23] The BBC has joined its commercial competitors by cutting local journalism and perhaps demonstrating to audiences across the country a lack of long-term commitment to them.

The BBC should be focussing on serving licence fee payers in underserved parts of the country with new and relevant content – delivered digitally. The current BBC regional television structure in England is an archaic throwback to the needs of BBC engineers to deliver television pictures to as many viewers as possible. This is highlighted in the service areas for regional television, for example how many people would place Carlisle in the North-East of England, or Northampton in East Anglia? Changes to digital distribution of local content are urgent. As *Netflix, Prime Video, Disney+* and other streaming services gain market share the BBC's

---

[23] See; Bauer closes dozens of regional radio stations in England and Wales, The Guardian, 31 August 2020. Available online at https://www.theguardian.com/media/2020/aug/31/merger-of-bauer-local-radio-stations-criticised-as-cultural-vandalism date accessed 5 September 2020; Who Owns the UK Media, Media Reform. Available online at https://www.mediareform.org.uk/wp-content/uploads/2019/03/execsumFINALonline2.pdf dated accessed 4 September 2020; UK newspaper publisher Reach to cut 550 jobs, Financial Times, 7 July 2020. Available online at https://www.ft.com/content/e36ab119-cccf-4159-8cbd-54f29e022520 date accessed 1 September 2020.

analogue regional TV services are losing penetration into their core audiences – even if they are holding up against their competitors in a shrinking sector. BARB figures show that between 2011 and 2021 the reach of BBC regional news programmes in England fell from 54 per cent to 34 per cent.[24] Similar falls have occurred in BBC local radio as Rajar reports a reach of 19 per cent in 2011 had fallen to 13 per cent in 2020.[25] Leaked unofficial figures show an uptick to BBC local radio reach during the Covid 19 lockdowns as listeners sought out local news. Indeed, it is the pandemic that has highlighted a need for a vigorous local news service and the BBC is uniquely placed – if it is brave enough to take advantage of a new digital literacy among consumers.

Embracing growing digital literacy.

In our homes we are increasingly going digital and on demand. The BBC's figures show that its digital services such as the *BBC iPlayer* notched up 1.7 billion streams in the first three months of 2021 and that *BBC Sounds* delivered 1.1 billion plays in 2020 – all while its local and regional journalism languishes in an analogue age. Only 16 years ago when the BBC drew up plans in 2005 for a local television service delivered to computers through the internet the reception to the idea inside the BBC was lukewarm. The local newspaper industry which saw a threat to its market share managed to kill off this potential challenge with the promise of their own video journalism – something that has failed to materialise.

Today after a considerable retrenchment in local journalism and a huge growth in digital literacy the media landscape is considerably changed. In the 2020s most people have access to and use smartphone technology and this penetration will improve into the decade. In young people saturation point has already been reached but the most remarkable adoption rates are in the 55-64's where over 80 per cent use a smartphone, up from under ten per cent in 2012.[26] This access to smartphones is perhaps one reason why new research by Ofcom found that the average UK adult spent 4 hours a day online in 2020.[27] The roll out of 5G will only make this technology

---

24 BBC Trust Service Review, BBC Local radio and Local News and Current Affairs in England, (BBC Trust, 2016), p.9.,
http://downloads.bbc.co.uk/bbctrust/assets/files/pdf/our_work/local_radio_news/performan ce_analysis.pdf date accessed 10 June 2021; and leaked BARB figures for May 2021.
25 RAJAR, Quarterly listening figures,
https://www.rajar.co.uk/listening/quarterly_listening.php, date accessed 10 June 2021.
26 S. O'Dea, Smartphone Usage in the UK by age, (Statista, 2020),
https://www.statista.com/statistics/300402/smartphone-usage-in-the-uk-by-age/ date accessed10 June 2021.

more ubiquitous and a major part of the BBC's levelling up agenda should be to mine its existing rich seams of local video, audio, text and picture content to connect at a personal and local level to licence fee payers.

New digital BBC local connections?

The success of the *BBC iPlayer, BBC Sounds* and *the BBC News* website proves there is an appetite for BBC content and coupled with the growing popularity of other streaming services such as *Netflix and Amazon Prime* shows that our media usage is becoming more personal and less reliant on fixed schedules. With the will to make it work and the regulatory ability to make it happen the BBC could repurpose its existing local and regional analogue content to produce local video, text and audio news direct to licence payers.

In England alone the BBC's 14 regional TV programmes and 36 local radio stations are producing an estimated 320,000 news stories a year. An 'App' using the digital power of the *BBC iPlayer* and *BBC Sounds* together with a judicious use of social media feeds could revolutionise and personalise the BBC's local offering. Given the importance of local news, accentuated during the Covid 19 pandemic, and the extensive digital literacy among consumers this service could help to drive up the relevance of the BBC among audiences who feel themselves to be underserved and distant from the BBC – both culturally and geographically.

Only a relevant BBC will survive.

One of the big policy platforms of the Johnson government is 'levelling up' and this chapter argues that the BBC has its own levelling up to do by breaking the London, metropolitan strangle hold of its policy and programmes. The BBC needs a step change in its dispersal of staff, programmes and decision making around the United Kingdom together with a fundamental reappraisal of its local and regional services for the smartphone consumers of the 2020s.

---

27 Ofcom, UK's Internet Use Surges to Record Levels, June 2020, https://www.ofcom.org.uk/about-ofcom/latest/media/media-releases/2020/uk-internet-use-surges date accessed 10 June 2021.

About the contributor.

Dr Liam McCarthy is an Honorary Fellow in the Department of History, Politics and International Relations at the University of Leicester. He worked for the BBC between 1978 and 2008 and was Editor of three BBC local stations in Leicester, Nottingham and Sheffield and Head of BBC Local Radio Training. In 2020 he completed a PhD at the University of Leicester which examined the social impact of the extensive Asian programming on BBC local radio in the 1970s and 1980s.

The Epilogue

The title of this chapter is deliberately double edged. Each night BBC radio used to end broadcasting with an Epilogue. I hope I am not ending this book with an epilogue to the BBC after 100 years of brilliant existence. It has simply become the best regarded and best broadcaster in the World in that time.

Britain's one world (soft)power.

The byword for good, honest, impartial journalism and great programmes of all genres.

The philistines are at the BBC gates. I am accustomed to many of 'my' BBC authors crying wolf about the future of the BBC. It is their default position. This time, I fear the wolves are about to huff and puff for a last time. The house is in mortal danger of falling down. The BBC is a wounded animal and the wildebeests are circling. They smell blood. BBC blood.

Political discourse in Britain has reached a new low since the 2016 Brexit Referendum. Dialogue is close to non-existent. The Populist Right are in full flow; they are waging a Culture War on all fronts against what they see as 'woke' ideas and institutions. The BBC their prime target. They regard it as full of bias, dangerous lefties, arrogant, out of touch with 'the people' and irrelevant in view of the rise of the 'California Streamers'.The (small) annual licence fee a 'poll tax' but one to be salami sliced away and replaced in 2027 or earlier. The house journal of the populists *The Daily Telegraph* carries anti BBC memes day by day. If they are right and know their readers, the BBC has had its day with the suburban bourgeoisie. They are not alone. With one or two exceptions, the British Press is solidly Right wing and nearly solidly anti-BBC.

All governments place their people at the top of the BBC. Richard Sharp is the newest — a chair implanted by Boris Johnson and by Sharp's protégé Rishi Sunak. There is a new Director General, Tim Davie, who was in his youth sympathetic to the Conservative cause, there is a Secretary of State Oliver Dowden ready to use his attack dog John Whittingdale to define 'public service' to the BBC , an arch populist Paul Dacre about to be shoe-horned into chairing *Ofcom* the broadcasting regulator, a Charter Mid-

Term Review coming up in 2022 with an end point for this charter of 2027. The omens are not good.

Normally, the BBC's friends are vocal in defence. The creative, liberal elite come out to bat in hordes. Not this time round. Barely a whimper. Defence committees come and defence committees go. Little avail.

The uber left regard the BBC as part of the hated 'MSM' (Mainstream Media), the various so called 'woke' communities-BAME, Gender, age and history revisionists and other interested groups-attack the Corporation for their own ends. The BBC can be seen to run scared of them. It should not.

There have also been far too many BBC own goals. The Bashir *'Panorama'* Affair is the most recent and the worst. Lord Dyson excoriated the Corporation in his report on the matter. It was a brilliant scoop ruined by the methods used to get it, cover up once those methods were discovered and, worst of all, the re-employment of the perpetuator in a senior BBC role. It was one big Xmas present for the BBC's enemies, especially in the printed press.

It was not the first in recent times. Harbouring Jimmy Savile, libelling Lord Mcalpine, falsely door-stepping Sir Cliff Richard did not paint the BBC in a good light. Thousands of hours of great journalism, years of brilliant programming ruined by mis-steps and worse their public revelation drip by drip. Transparency always pays in the end.

What is the answer? Back to basics. Think about the purposes of the BBC, what it does and how it is financed. Think of the value it offers audiences and whether that could be enhanced or improved. Are incremental subscriptions for services such as sport and music such a bad idea? The BBC brand is much more potent than the *Netflix* one. Use it. It guarantees programme quality and should guaranteed integrity and truth. The status quo ante is not an alternative.

Think of the scope and range of the BBC.Is it too wide, too diffuse? Should some services or extras be deemed surplus to the central mission (My candidate would be the BBC Orchestras)? Should others-like the World Service-be financed differently?

Should the BBC better use the greatest advertising medium invented - Television – better to sell itself? Should it simply continue to make brilliant programmes as the guarantor of longevity?

The solution lies in its hands and that of the predators.

Tim Davie does not want to be the 17th and last BBC Director General.

The History Boy become History himself.

Bite-Sized Public Affairs Books are designed to provide insights and stimulating ideas that affect us all in, for example, journalism, social policy, education, government and politics.

They are deliberately short, easy to read, and authoritative books written by people who are either on the front line or who are informed observers. They are designed to stimulate discussion, thought and innovation in all areas of public affairs. They are all firmly based on personal experience and direct involvement and engagement.

The most successful people all share an ability to focus on what really matters, keeping things simple and understandable. When we are faced with a new challenge most of us need quick guidance on what matters most, from people who have been there before and who can show us where to start.

They can be read straight through at one easy sitting and then referred to as necessary – a trusted repository of hard-won experience.

Bite-Sized Books Catalogue

We publish Business Books, Life-Style Books, Public Affairs Books, including our Brexit Books, Fiction – both short form and long form – and Children's Fiction.

To see our full range of books, please go to

https://bite-sizedbooks.com/

Printed in Great Britain
by Amazon

86136924R00079